Mum's Favourite Bakes

Mum's Favourite Bakes

Bounty
BOOKS

Mum's Favourite Bakes

Publisher: Polly Manguel
Editorial and Design Manager: Emma Hill
Editor: Jane Birch
Designer: Chris Bell/cbdesign
Production Manager: Neil Randles

Published in 2013 by Bounty Books,
a division of Octopus Publishing Group Ltd
Endeavour House, 189 Shaftesbury Avenue,
London WC2H 8JY
www.octopusbooks.co.uk

An Hachette UK Company
www.hachette.co.uk

ISBN: 978-0-753723-43-2

Printed and bound in China.

Contents

Baking Basics

Baking is immensely rewarding and you'll find something for every occasion in this collection of traditional family favourites. Here are a few tips and techniques to ensure baking success every time.

BAKING EQUIPMENT
Some of this equipment, such as accurate scales and a cooling rack, is essential whatever you are baking and some, like cookie cutters and a rolling pin, will only be needed for certain types of baking.

Scales Good measuring scales are vital when it comes to baking. Digital add-and-weigh scales are the easiest and clearest to use as the weight of ingredients is shown with pinpoint accuracy.

Measuring spoons A set of measuring spoons – from ¼ teaspoon up to 1 tablespoon – is invaluable for measuring out ingredients such as spices, baking powder and vanilla extract. When measuring dry ingredients, all spoonfuls should be level unless otherwise specified in the recipe.

Measuring jug Perfect for measuring liquids accurately, a glass one is easier to read and will last longer than plastic.

Mixing bowls These can be glass, plastic, china or stainless steel and you will probably need at least three of different sizes, including one extra-large bowl.

Cooling rack This is needed to cool cakes and breads after baking so that the steam can escape and the bases don't go soggy.

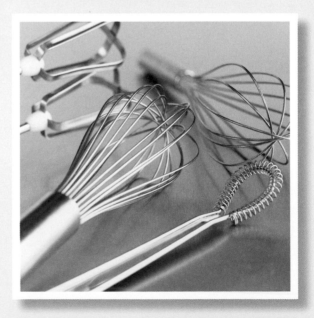

Whisks A hand-held electric whisk will make life much easier when it comes to mixing together ingredients. Alternatively, balloon whisks and rotary whisks can be used but mixing will take longer and be much harder work.

Rolling pin A wooden rolling pin without handles is the best choice.

Spatula A flexible plastic spatula is useful when folding in flour or whisked egg whites as well as for scraping cake mixture into cake tins.

Sieves Invest in at least two strong, stainless steel or plastic sieves; a larger one for sifting dry ingredients, such as flour, and a smaller on for sifting icing sugar over the top of baked cakes.

Pastry brush For greasing cake tins and glazing tops of scones, pies and buns.

Baking sheets You'll need two of these when making cookies, biscuits, meringues, scones and rolls. They're also useful for providing a secure base under flexible silicone bakeware.

Cutters For cutting out biscuits, cookies, little tarts and scones, these are available in a wide variety of shapes. For best results the cutter should be sharp so metal ones tend to be better than plastic.

Tins Cake and tart tins come in a variety of shapes, sizes and materials. Look for tins made from heavy-gauge metal as they are less likely to warp or have hot spots. Flexible silicone moulds, available in an array of eye-catching colours, are easy to clean and easy to use as cakes can simply be popped out of them. Always make sure you choose use the correct size tin, as specified in the recipe.

Piping bags and nozzles These are useful for piping whipped cream and icing onto cakes, cookies and muffins. Nylon bags tend to be more flexible and easier to use than thicker plastic ones.

Paper cupcake and muffin cases Rather then greasing muffin and cupcake tins, paper cases save time and washing up and come in a great range of novelty designs, sizes and colours.

CAKES

Cakes should be an even colour all over when cooked. Sponge cakes will spring back when gently pressed with your fingertips. A fine skewer pressed into the middle of larger cakes should come out clean and dry.

Preparing cake tins To line cake tins use greaseproof or baking paper and brush the tin's base and sides with melted butter before you start lining. Most cakes need a completely lined tin – both base and sides lined with paper – but some only need the base lined. See the individual recipes for instructions on how to line the tins.

BREAD

Yeast is the most important ingredient when it comes to making bread. Fast-action dried yeast is the easiest to use. Choose strong flour, sometimes called bread flour, for breadmaking as it has a higher gluten content for added stretch.

Kneading This is essential to mix and activate the yeast and to help stretch the gluten in the flour so that the bread will rise. Turn the dough out onto a lightly floured surface. Stretch it by pushing the front half away with the heel of one hand while holding the back of the dough with the other hand. Fold the stretched part back on itself, give it a quarter turn and repeat for 5 more minutes, until the dough has been fully turned several times and is a smooth and elastic ball.

Knocking back After bread dough has been kneaded it should be placed in an oiled bowl, covered with a clean tea towel or oiled clingfilm and left in a warm place until it has doubled in size. This is called proving. Then remove the clingfilm or tea towel and 'knock back' the dough by punching it with your fist to deflate it. Then turn it out onto a lightly floured surface and knead well.

Is it ready? Bread should be well risen, golden brown and sound hollow when tapped with the fingertips. Test the top then turn out on to a wire rack and tap the base of the bread to double check it is done. If the base feels a little soft, return it to the oven, placing it directly on to the oven shelf, and check again in 5 minutes.

PASTRY

The secret to making good pastry is to keep everything cool, use a light touch and to handle the pastry as little as possible. Add just enough water to mix; too much and the pastry will be sticky and the texture will be hard when baked.

Lining a tin with pastry Roll out the pastry on a lightly floured surface a little larger than the tin. Lift over the rolling pin and drape into the tin. Press over the base and sides of the tin with your fingertips, taking care where the sides meet the base. Trim off the excess pastry with a knife a little above the top of the tin to allow for shrinkage.

Baking blind This refers to baking the pastry case on its own before the filling is added. Line the tart case with a piece of greaseproof or nonstick baking paper large enough to cover the base and sides of the tart. Add a generous layer of baking beans (available from cookware stores and large supermarkets) or use dried pasta or pulses. Place the tart on a baking sheet and bake in a preheated oven as directed in the recipe.

Shortcrust Pastry

Makes 470 g (15 oz)

250 g (8 oz) plain flour
125 g (4 oz) half butter and half white
  vegetable fat or lard, or all butter, diced
2½–3 tablespoons iced water
salt

Add the flour and a pinch of salt to a large mixing bowl. Add the fats and rub them into the flour with your fingertips, or use a freestanding electric mixer, until the mixture resembles fine crumbs.

Gradually mix in just enough water to enable the crumbs to be squeezed together to form a soft, but not sticky, dough. Knead very lightly until smooth, then roll out on a lightly floured surface and use to line a tart case or top a pie.

Sweet shortcrust pastry Add 50 g (2 oz) caster sugar to the bowl with the flour and salt and use 125 g (4 oz) butter instead of a mix of butter and white vegetable fat or lard. Continue as above.

Flavour variations Try adding 1 teaspoon dry English mustard, a few chopped fresh herbs or 40 g (1½ oz) freshly grated Parmesan or Cheddar cheese.

Biscuits & Cookies

Thumbprint Cookies
Oat & Ginger Crunchies
Almond Biscuits
Florentines
Chunky Monkeys
Traditional Shortbread
Lavender Shortbread
Ginger Snaps
Chocolate Chip Cookies
Walnut & White Chocolate Cookies
Citrus Cream Clouds
Lemon Biscuits
Vanilla & Sesame Wafers
Peanut Butter Cookies
Quick Hazelnut Melts
Fig & Date Rolls
Chocolate Kisses

Thumbprint Cookies

Makes 14
Preparation time 20 minutes
Cooking time 20 minutes

125 g (4 oz) unsalted butter,
    softened
50 g (2 oz) light brown sugar
1 egg, separated
½ teaspoon ground mixed
    spice
100 g (3½ oz) plain flour
75 g (3 oz) slivered almonds,
    crushed
5 tablespoons strawberry or
    raspberry jam
icing sugar, for dusting
    (optional)

Beat the butter and brown sugar until creamy. Add the egg yolk, ground mixed spice and flour and mix to form a soft dough. Lightly beat the egg white to break it up and tip it on to a plate. Scatter the almonds on a separate plate.

Shape the dough into small balls, 3 cm (1¼ inches) in diameter, and roll them first in the egg white and then in the almonds until well coated.

Place the balls on a greased baking sheet, spaced slightly apart, and flatten slightly. Bake in a preheated oven, 180°C (350°F), Gas Mark 4, for 10 minutes, then remove from the oven. Allow to cool a little, then lightly flour your thumb and make a thumbprint in the centre of each cookie. Spoon a little jam into each cavity and return the cookies to the oven for an extra 10 minutes or until pale golden. Transfer to a wire rack to cool.

Dust the edges of the cookies with icing sugar, if liked. They will keep, in an airtight container in a cool place, for a few days.

Oat & Ginger Crunchies

Makes 25
Preparation time 20 minutes
Cooking time 24–30 minutes

100 g (3½ oz) butter
1 tablespoon golden syrup
100 g (3½ oz) caster sugar
1 teaspoon bicarbonate of
    soda
1 teaspoon ground ginger
2 tablespoons ready-chopped
    glacé ginger
100 g (3½ oz) plain wholemeal
    flour
125 g (4 oz) porridge oats

Put the butter, syrup and sugar in a saucepan and heat gently, stirring until the butter has melted and the sugar dissolved. Remove the pan from the heat then stir in the bicarbonate of soda, ground and chopped ginger. Add the flour and oats and mix well.

Spoon heaped teaspoons of the mixture on to 3 lightly greased baking sheets, leaving a little space between for the biscuits to spread during cooking.

Cook one baking sheet at a time in the centre of a preheated oven, 180°C (350°F), Gas Mark 4, for 8–10 minutes until the biscuits are craggy and golden. Leave to harden for 1–2 minutes then loosen and transfer to a wire rack to cool. Store in an airtight tin for up to 3 days.

Almond Biscuits

Makes about 14
Preparation time 20 minutes
Cooking time 10 minutes

150 g (5 oz) ground almonds
1 tablespoon plain flour
175 g (6 oz) caster sugar, plus
   extra for coating
½ teaspoon baking powder
1 egg white
½ teaspoon vanilla extract

Combine the almonds, flour, sugar and baking powder in a large bowl. Beat the egg white in a separate bowl until it holds its shape and has a consistency resembling shaving foam. Fold into the almond mixture. Add the vanilla extract and stir to combine thoroughly.

Dust a work surface with sugar. Roll 1 tablespoon of the biscuit dough in the palm of your hands to make a sausage shape about 6 cm (2½ inches) long. Roll in the sugar, then place on a baking sheet lined with baking parchment. Repeat with the remaining dough to make about 14 biscuits. Make sure you leave plenty of space between each biscuit, as they spread during cooking.

Bake the biscuits in a preheated oven, 200°C (400°F), Gas Mark 6, for 10 minutes until lightly golden.

Florentines

Makes 48
Preparation time 30 minutes,
  plus cooling and setting
Cooking time 40 minutes

150 g (5 oz) butter
175 g (6 oz) caster sugar
4 tablespoons double cream
75 g (3 oz) mixed peel,
  chopped
50 g (2 oz) glacé cherries,
  chopped
50 g (2 oz) flaked almonds
40 g (1½ oz) dried cranberries
25 g (1 oz) pine nuts
50 g (2 oz) plain flour
150 g (5 oz) plain dark
  chocolate
150 g (5 oz) white chocolate

Heat the butter and sugar gently in a pan until the butter is melted. Increase the heat and bring to the boil. Immediately remove the pan from the heat, add the cream, mixed peel, cherries, almonds, cranberries, pine nuts and flour. Stir well until evenly combined.

Grease 2 large baking sheets and line with nonstick baking paper. Drop 12 heaped teaspoonfuls (a quarter of the mixture) on to each of the baking sheets, leaving a 5 cm (2 inch) gap for spreading. Bake in a preheated oven, 180°C (350°F), Gas Mark 4, for 7 minutes.

Remove the baking sheets from the oven. Using a 7 cm (3 inch) cookie cutter, carefully drag the edges of the biscuits into neat rounds so that they are about 5 cm (2 inches) across. Bake for a further 3–4 minutes until golden around the edges. Remove from the oven and leave for 2 minutes. Use a palette knife to transfer the biscuits to baking paper and leave to cool. Repeat with the remaining mixture.

Melt the plain dark and white chocolate in separate bowls over pans of simmering water (see page 53). Spoon the melted chocolate into separate piping bags and drizzle over the biscuits. Leave to set.

Chunky Monkeys

Makes 12
Preparation time 10 minutes
Cooking time 10–12 minutes

200 g (7 oz) plain flour
1 teaspoon bicarbonate
    of soda
125 g (4 oz) sugar
125 g (4 oz) butter, cut into
    cubes
1 egg
1 tablespoon milk
150 g (5 oz) white chocolate,
    roughly chopped
75 g (3 oz) glacé cherries,
    roughly chopped

Put the flour, bicarbonate of soda and sugar in a bowl and mix through. Add the butter and rub in with the fingertips until the mixture resembles breadcrumbs.

Beat together the egg and milk in a separate bowl. Add the chopped chocolate and glacé cherries, then mix into the flour mixture and stir well until smooth.

Drop heaped spoonfuls of the cookie mixture, well spaced apart, on to a greased baking sheet and bake in a preheated oven, 180°C (350°F), Gas Mark 4, for 10–12 minutes until lightly golden. Leave to harden on the tray for 2 minutes, then slide off on to a wire rack or plate to cool.

Traditional Shortbread

Makes 8 pieces
Preparation time 15 minutes,
  plus chilling
Cooking time 45–60 minutes

250 g (8 oz) plain flour
125 g (4 oz) rice flour or
  ground rice
125 g (4 oz) caster sugar, plus
  extra for dusting
pinch of salt
250 g (8 oz) unsalted butter,
  softened

Sift the 2 flours (or flour and rice), sugar and salt into a mixing bowl. Rub in the butter with your fingertips. When the mixture starts to bind, gather it with one hand into a ball. Knead it on a lightly floured surface to a soft, smooth, pliable dough.

Put the dough in a 20 cm (8 inch) flan ring set on a greased baking sheet. Press it out with your knuckles to fit the ring. Mark the shortbread into 8 pieces using the back of a knife. Prick right through to the baking sheet with a fork in a neat pattern. Cover and chill for at least 1 hour before baking, to firm it up.

Bake in a preheated oven, 150°C (300°F), Gas Mark 2, for 45–60 minutes, or until the shortbread is a pale biscuit colour but still soft. Remove the shortbread from the oven and leave to cool and shrink before removing the ring, then dust lightly with caster sugar. When cold, cut into 8 pieces. It will keep, in an airtight container in a cool place, for a few days.

Lavender Shortbread

Makes 18–20
Preparation time 15 minutes,
  plus chilling
Cooking time 15–20 minutes

125 g (4 oz) caster sugar
4 dried lavender flowers,
  natural and unsprayed
225 g (7½ oz) unsalted butter,
  softened
225 g (7½ oz) plain flour
120 g (4 oz) ground rice
pinch of salt

To decorate
extra caster sugar and dried
  lavender flowers

Line 2 baking sheets with greaseproof paper. Put the sugar and lavender flowers in a food processor and process for about 10 seconds. Cream the butter and lavender sugar together in a bowl until pale and fluffy, then stir in the flour, ground rice and salt until the mixture resembles fine breadcrumbs.

Using your hands, gather the dough together and knead until it forms a ball. Roll the dough into a log, then shape it into a long, straight-edged block about 5 cm (2 inches) in diameter. Wrap the dough in cling film and chill in the refrigerator for about 30 minutes, or until firm.

Slice the dough into 5 mm (¼ inch) squares and place on the prepared baking sheets. Bake in a preheated oven, 190°C (375°F), Gas Mark 5, for 15–20 minutes, or until pale golden. Remove from the oven and sprinkle the shortbread immediately with extra caster sugar. Leave to cool on the baking sheets for 10 minutes, then transfer to a wire rack and leave to cool completely. Decorate with extra lavender flowers before serving.

Ginger Snaps

Makes 40–44
Preparation time 15 minutes
Cooking time 13–15 minutes

375 g (12 oz) self-raising flour
1 tablespoon ground ginger
1 teaspoon bicarbonate of
   soda
pinch of salt
200 g (7 oz) granulated sugar,
   plus extra for dusting
125 g (4 oz) unsalted butter,
4 tablespoons black treacle,
1 tablespoon milk
1 egg, beaten

Sift the flour, ginger, bicarbonate of soda and salt into a bowl and stir in the sugar. Put the butter and treacle in a saucepan and heat gently until the butter is melted, remove from the heat and leave to cool for 15 minutes.

Beat the cooled butter mixture into the dry ingredients with the milk and egg and mix together until evenly combined, then knead briefly until smooth.

Take 15 g (½ oz) pieces of dough and roll them into balls. Flatten them into 5 cm (2 inch) discs and place them, slightly apart, on 2 large, lightly oiled baking sheets.

Sprinkle the biscuits with a little granulated sugar and bake in a preheated oven, 180°C (350°F), Gas Mark 4, for 13–15 minutes until evenly browned. Leave to cool on the baking sheets for 2 minutes then transfer to a wire rack to cool. Repeat with the remaining dough to make 40–44 biscuits.

Chocolate Chip Cookies

Makes 25
Preparation time 10 minutes
Cooking time 15–20 minutes

125 g (4 oz) butter, softened
50 g (2 oz) light soft brown
   sugar
1 egg, beaten
150 g (5 oz) self-raising flour
125 g (4 oz) plain chocolate,
   finely chopped

Grease a baking sheet lightly. Put the butter and sugar in a mixing bowl and beat together with a wooden spoon until light and fluffy. Beat in the egg, then sift in the flour. Add the chocolate pieces and mix thoroughly.

Put 25 teaspoonfuls of the mixture slightly apart on the baking sheet and bake in a preheated oven, 180°C (350°F), Gas Mark 4, for 15–20 minutes until golden brown.

Remove from the oven and leave the cookies on the baking sheet for 1 minute, then transfer to a wire rack and allow to cool.

Walnut & White Chocolate Cookies

Makes about 25
Preparation time 15 minutes,
  plus cooling
Cooking time 12–15 minutes

1 egg
150 g (5 oz) soft light brown
  sugar
2 tablespoons caster sugar
1 teaspoon vanilla extract
125 ml (4 fl oz) vegetable oil
65 g (2½ oz) plain flour
3 tablespoons self-raising
  flour
¼ teaspoon ground cinnamon
25 g (1 oz) shredded coconut
175 g (6 oz) walnuts, toasted
  and chopped
125 g (4 oz) white chocolate
  chips

Grease 2 baking sheets and line with nonstick baking paper. In a bowl, beat the egg and sugars together until light and creamy. Stir in the vanilla extract and oil. Sift in the flours and cinnamon, then add the coconut, walnuts and chocolate and mix well with a wooden spoon.

Form rounded tablespoonfuls of the mixture into balls and place on the prepared baking sheets, pressing the mixture together with your fingertips if it is crumbly.

Bake in a preheated oven, 180°C (350°F), Gas Mark 4, for 12–15 minutes or until golden. Leave to cool slightly on the sheets, then transfer to a wire rack to cool completely.

Citrus Cream Clouds

Makes 18
Preparation time 25 minutes, plus chilling
Cooking time 5–8 minutes

180 g (6 oz) unsalted butter, softened
1 teaspoon finely grated lime zest
80 g (3 oz) icing sugar
225 g (7½ oz) plain flour
40 g (1½ oz) cornflour

Filling
125 g (4 oz) unsalted butter, softened
1 teaspoon vanilla extract
1 teaspoon finely grated orange zest
1 teaspoon finely grated lemon zest
160 g (5½ oz) icing sugar, sifted, plus extra for dusting

For the dough, beat the butter, lime zest and icing sugar together in a bowl until smooth and creamy. Stir in the flour and cornflour to make a dough, then knead until smooth. Wrap the dough in cling film and chill in the refrigerator for 30 minutes, or until firm.

Line 2 or 3 baking sheets with nonstick baking paper. Roll out half the dough between two sheets of nonstick baking paper. Using a flower-shaped biscuit cutter or a cutter of your choice, cut out 18 x 4 cm (18 x 1½ inch) shapes.

Add any trimmings of dough to the remaining pastry, roll out as before and cut out 18 x 6 cm (18 x 2½ inch) shapes. Place the dough shapes about 2.5 cm (1 inch) apart on the prepared baking sheets.

Bake in a preheated oven, 180°C (350°F), Gas Mark 4, for about 5–6 minutes for the small shapes and 7–8 minutes for the large shapes, or until lightly browned. Transfer to a wire rack and leave to cool completely.

Put all the filling ingredients in a bowl and beat together until smooth and creamy. Either pipe or spread the filling onto each of the larger biscuits. Top each one with a smaller biscuit. Dust with sifted icing sugar to serve.

Lemon Biscuits

Makes 18–20
Preparation time 15 minutes,
  plus cooling
Cooking time 15–20 minutes

125 g (4 oz) unsalted butter,
  diced and softened
125 g (4 oz) caster sugar
2 egg yolks
2 teaspoons grated lemon
  rind
150 g (5 oz) plain flour
100 g (3½ oz) coarse cornmeal
saffron, to sprinkle (optional)
icing sugar, for dusting

Line a baking sheet with nonstick baking paper. In a bowl, beat the butter and sugar together until light and fluffy. Mix in the egg yolks, lemon rind, flour and cornmeal until a soft dough forms.

Roll out the dough on a lightly floured surface to 1 cm (½ inch) thick. Using a 6 cm (2½ inch) round cutter, cut out rounds from the dough, re-rolling the trimmings. Transfer to the prepared baking sheet, then sprinkle with saffron, if liked, and bake in a preheated oven, 160°C (325°F), Gas Mark 3, for 15–20 minutes or until lightly golden. Transfer to a wire rack to cool, then dust with icing sugar.

Vanilla & Sesame Wafers

Makes 48
Preparation time 20 minutes
Cooking time 15–18 minutes

50 g (2 oz) sesame seeds
65 g (2½ oz) plain flour
½ teaspoon baking powder
125 g (4 oz) butter, softened
125 g (4 oz) soft brown sugar
1 egg
1 teaspoon vanilla extract

Spread the sesame seeds in a shallow tin and bake in a preheated oven, 160°C (325°F), Gas Mark 3, stirring occasionally, for 6–8 minutes, or until lightly toasted. Set aside.

Sift the flour, baking powder and salt into a bowl, then set aside.

Cream the butter and sugar in a mixing bowl until light and fluffy. Beat in the egg. Add the vanilla extract and mix well. Gradually add the flour mixture until just blended. Add the toasted sesame seeds and stir until well combined.

Place rounded teaspoonfuls, about 5 cm (2 inches) apart, on 3 large greased baking sheets. Bake in the oven for 9–10 minutes or until the biscuits are lightly browned. They are very fragile when they first come out of the oven so leave them on the baking sheets to cool for about 1 minute, then carefully transfer to wire racks to cool completely.

Peanut Butter Cookies

Makes 32
Preparation time 10 minutes
Cooking time 12 minutes

125 g (4 oz) unsalted butter,
  softened
150 g (5 oz) soft brown sugar
125 g (4 oz) crunchy peanut
  butter
1 egg, lightly beaten
150 g (5 oz) plain flour
½ teaspoon baking powder
125 g (4 oz) unsalted peanuts

Beat together the butter and sugar in a bowl or food processor until pale and creamy. Add the peanut butter, egg, flour and baking powder and stir together until combined. Stir in the peanuts.

Drop large teaspoonfuls of the mixture on to 3 large, lightly oiled baking sheets, leaving 5 cm (2 inch) gaps between each one for them to spread during cooking.

Flatten the mounds slightly with a fork and bake in a preheated oven, 190°C (375°F), Gas Mark 5, for 12 minutes until golden around the edges. Leave to cool on the baking sheets for 2 minutes, then transfer to a wire rack to cool completely.

Quick Hazelnut Melts

Makes 20
Preparation time 10 minutes
Cooking time 15 minutes

50 g (2 oz) blanched hazelnuts
125 g (4 oz) butter, softened
50 g (2 oz) caster sugar
150 g (5 oz) plain flour

Grind the hazelnuts in a food processor until fairly smooth, but still retaining a little texture. Dry-fry in a heavy-based frying pan over a low heat until evenly golden. Tip into a bowl and stir until cool.

Blend the butter and sugar together in the processor until creamy. Add the flour and cooled nuts and process again to make a soft dough.

Take walnut-size pieces of the dough and shape into rolls, then pat into flat ovals. Place on a greased baking sheet and bake in a preheated oven, 190°C (375°F), Gas Mark 5, for 12 minutes, until just golden. Cool on a wire rack.

Fig & Date Rolls

Makes 24
Preparation time 25 minutes,
  plus cooling
Cooking time 20–25 minutes

125 g (4 oz) unsalted butter,
  softened
75 g (3 oz) caster sugar
1 teaspoon ground cinnamon
1 egg, lightly beaten
75 g (3 oz) ground almonds
225 g (7½ oz) plain flour

Filling
300 g (10 oz) dried figs, finely
  chopped
80 g (3 oz) stoned dried
  dates, finely chopped
finely grated zest of 1 lemon
100 g (3½ oz) caster sugar

For the filling, put all the ingredients together with 125 ml (4 fl oz) of water in a saucepan and stir over a gentle heat until the sugar has dissolved. Simmer, uncovered, for about 15 minutes, or until the mixture is thick and pulpy. Remove the pan from the heat and set aside to cool.

For the dough, beat the butter, sugar, cinnamon and egg together in a bowl. Stir in the ground almonds and flour, mixing to make a dough. Knead the dough lightly, then divide it into four equal portions. Wrap each portion in cling film and chill in the refrigerator for 30 minutes.

Roll out each portion of dough between 2 sheets of nonstick baking paper to form a rectangle about 10 x 20 cm (4 x 5 inches) in size. Spread a quarter of the filling along each rectangle, leaving a 1 cm (½ inch) border around the edges. Fold the long sides over the filling to meet in the centre and press gently together. Tuck the ends of each rectangle under.

Place the rolls, seam-side down, on nonstick baking sheets. Bake in a preheated oven, 180°C (350°F), Gas Mark 4, for 20–25 minutes, or until lightly browned. Transfer to a wire rack to cool. When cold, cut into slices. These biscuits keep well in an airtight container for several days.

Chocolate Kisses

Makes 20–25
Preparation time 15 minutes,
  plus cooling and chilling
Cooking time 15 minutes

2 large egg whites
¼ teaspoon cream of tartar
225 g (7½ oz) caster sugar
4 tablespoons cocoa powder,
  sifted
150 g (5 oz) ground almonds
1 teaspoon almond extract

Filling
100 g (3½ oz) plain dark
  chocolate, chopped
125 ml (4 fl oz) double cream

Whisk the egg whites and cream of tartar in a grease-free bowl until stiff, then gradually whisk in the sugar, 1 tablespoon at a time, until the mixture thickens. Fold in the cocoa powder, almonds and almond extract with a metal spoon until evenly combined.

Spoon the mixture into a piping bag fitted with a large star nozzle and pipe 2.5 cm (1 inch) rosettes onto 2 large, lined baking sheets (you should have 40–50 rosettes, depending on the size).

Bake in a preheated oven, 150°C (300°F), Gas Mark 2, for 15 minutes until the biscuits are just set. Remove from the oven and leave to cool completely on the baking sheets.

Melt the chocolate with the cream in a bowl over a pan of simmering water (see page 53). Cool and then chill for 30 minutes. Whip the chocolate mix until thick and fluffy and use to sandwich the biscuits together to make kisses.

Little Cakes & Bakes

Chocolate Caramel Shortbread

Prune & Sunflower Squares

Orange & Lemon Cupcakes

Rhubarb Crumble Cupcakes

Vanilla Cupcakes

Malty Raisin Cupcakes

Sultana & Ginger Cupcakes

Chocolate Orange Cupcakes

Rock Buns

Banana & Raisin Flapjacks

Blondies

Chocolate Mocha Brownies

Chocolate Meringues

Fresh Lemon Slices

Madeleines

Chocolate Caramel Shortbread

Makes 20
Preparation time 25 minutes,
  plus cooling and setting
Cooking time 40 minutes

200 g (7 oz) plain flour
50 g (2 oz) cocoa powder
75 g (3 oz) golden caster
  sugar
175 g (6 oz) butter
200 g (7 oz) white chocolate

Caramel
750 g (1½ lb) condensed milk
100 g (3½ oz) light
  muscovado sugar
100 g (3½ oz) butter

Blend the flour, cocoa powder, sugar and butter in a food processor until the mixture forms crumbs, then pulse a little more until it forms a ball. Turn on to a lightly floured surface and knead until it is smooth and well combined.

Grease and line a 30 x 20 cm (12 x 8 inch) Swiss roll tin. Press the mixture into the tin and bake in a preheated oven, 180°C (350°F), Gas Mark 4, for 20 minutes until firm to the touch.

Heat the condensed milk, sugar and butter in a nonstick pan, stirring continuously, for about 15 minutes until the mixture is thick and fudgy. Pour on top of the chocolate shortbread, smooth over and cool.

Melt the white chocolate in a bowl over a pan of simmering water (see page 51) and pour it over the caramel. Leave to set at room temperature, then cut into 20 squares.

Prune & Sunflower Squares

Makes 16
Preparation time 25 minutes
Cooking time 30–35 minutes

250 g (8 oz) ready-to-eat
    stoned prunes, roughly
    chopped
1 teaspoon vanilla essence
200 ml (7 fl oz) water
150 g (5 oz) butter
100 g (3½ oz) caster sugar
2 tablespoons golden syrup
100 g (3½ oz) self-raising flour
150 g (5 oz) porridge oats
40 g (1½ oz) sunflower seeds

To decorate
3 tablespoons porridge oats
2 tablespoons sunflower
    seeds

Put the prunes, vanilla and water in a small saucepan. Simmer, uncovered, for 5 minutes until soft and pulpy and the water has been absorbed.

Heat the butter, sugar and syrup in a larger saucepan until melted. Stir in the flour, oats and seeds and mix until well combined.

Spoon three-quarters of the mixture into a 20 cm (8 inch) shallow square cake tin lined with nonstick baking paper. Press into an even layer then cover with the cooked prunes. Sprinkle the remaining oat mixture over the top in a thin layer then decorate with the extra oats and sunflower seeds. Bake in a preheated oven, 180°C (350°F), Gas Mark 4, for 25–30 minutes until golden brown.

Leave to cool in the tin for 10 minutes then mark into 16 squares and leave to cool completely. Lift the flapjack out of the tin using the lining paper, peel off the paper and separate the squares. Store in an airtight tin for up to 3 days.

Orange & Lemon Cupcakes

Makes 12
Preparation time 20 minutes,
  plus cooling and setting
Cooking time 15–20 minutes

50 g (2 oz) lightly salted
  butter, softened
100 g (3½ oz) caster sugar
2 eggs
100 g (3½ oz) self-raising flour
1 tablespoon finely grated
  lemon rind
2 tablespoons orange flower
  water
2–3 tablespoons milk

Icing
200 g (7 oz) icing sugar, sifted
1½ tablespoons orange juice
1½ tablespoons lemon juice
yellow and orange food
  colouring

To decorate
finely pared orange and
  lemon rind coated in
  caster sugar

Line a 12-section bun tray with paper or foil cake cases. Put the butter, caster sugar, eggs, flour and grated lemon rind in a bowl and beat with a hand-held electric whisk until smooth.

Add the orange flower water and enough milk to give a good dropping consistency. Divide the cake mixture between the cake cases.

Bake in a preheated oven, 200°C (400°F), Gas Mark 6, for 15–20 minutes or until risen and golden. Transfer to a wire rack to cool.

Slice the risen tops off the cakes. Mix half the icing sugar with the orange juice in one bowl and the other half with the lemon juice in another bowl. Dot a tiny amount of the relevant food colouring into each one and stir well until you have 2 pastel-coloured icings.

Pour a small amount of the orange icing over 6 of the cakes using a teaspoon to cover the surface evenly. Repeat with the remaining cakes, using the yellow icing. Decorate with the sugar-coated orange and lemon rind, pressing it on lightly. Leave to set completely.

Rhubarb Crumble Cupcakes

Makes 12
Preparation time 20 minutes,
  plus cooling
Cooking time 45 minutes–
1 hour

sunflower oil, for brushing
275 g (9 oz) young rhubarb,
  trimmed and cut into
  1 cm (½ inch) lengths
200 g (7 oz) light
muscovado sugar
175 g (6 oz) lightly salted
  butter, softened
225 g (7½ oz) self-raising flour
1 teaspoon baking powder
½ teaspoon ground cinnamon
3 eggs
3 tablespoons flaked almonds
icing sugar, for dusting

Line a 12-section bun tray with paper or foil cake cases. Lightly brush a foil-lined baking sheet with oil and scatter with the rhubarb. Sprinkle with 25 g (1 oz) of the muscovado sugar and bake in a preheated oven, 200°C (400°F), Gas Mark 6, for 20–30 minutes or until tender and beginning to darken around the edges. Leave to cool. Reduce the oven to 180°C (350°F), Gas Mark 4.

Put a further 150 g (5 oz) of the sugar, 150 g (5 oz) of the butter, 175 g (6 oz) of the flour, the baking powder, cinnamon and eggs in a bowl and beat with a hand-held electric whisk for about a minute until light and creamy. Divide the cake mixture between the cake cases, spreading it fairly level, and top with the rhubarb pieces.

Put the remaining butter and flour in a food processor and process until the mixture resembles coarse breadcrumbs. Add the remaining muscovado sugar and process briefly until mixed. Scatter over the cakes and sprinkle with the almonds.

Bake for 25–30 minutes, until risen and golden. Transfer to a wire rack to cool. Serve dusted with icing sugar.

Vanilla Cupcakes

Makes 12
Preparation time 10 minutes
Cooking time 20 minutes

150 g (5 oz) lightly salted
 butter, softened
150 g (5 oz) caster sugar
175 g (6 oz) self-raising flour
3 eggs
1 teaspoon vanilla extract

Line a 12-section bun tray with paper or foil cake cases, or stand 12 silicone cases on a baking sheet.

Put all the cake ingredients in a bowl and beat with a hand-held electric whisk for 1–2 minutes until light and creamy. Divide the cake mixture between the cake cases.

Bake in a preheated oven, 180°C (350°F), Gas Mark 4, for 20 minutes or until risen and just firm to the touch. Transfer to a wire rack to cool.

Malty Raisin Cupcakes

Makes 12
Preparation time 10 minutes,
  plus standing
Cooking time 20 minutes

40 g (1½ oz) lightly salted
  butter, cut into pieces
75 g (3 oz) bran flakes
225 ml (8 fl oz) milk
100 g (3½ oz) light
  muscovado sugar
125 g (4 oz) raisins
125 g (4 oz) self-raising flour
½ teaspoon baking powder

Line a 12-section bun tray with paper or foil cake cases.
Put the butter and bran flakes in a heatproof bowl.

Bring the milk almost to the boil in a saucepan and pour
into the bowl. Leave to stand for 10–15 minutes until the
bran flakes are very soft and the mixture has cooled slightly,
then stir in the sugar and raisins.

Sift the flour and baking powder into the bowl and then
stir until just mixed. Divide the cake mixture between the
cake cases.

Bake in a preheated oven, 180°C (350°F), Gas Mark 4, for
20 minutes or until slightly risen and just firm to the touch.
Transfer to a wire rack to cool.

Sultana & Ginger Cupcakes

Makes 12
Preparation time 15 minutes,
    plus cooling
Cooking time 20 minutes

50 g (2 oz) piece of fresh root
    ginger
125 g (4 oz) lightly salted
    butter, softened
125 g (4 oz) caster sugar
2 eggs
150 g (5 oz) self-raising flour
½ teaspoon baking powder
½ teaspoon vanilla extract
50 g (2 oz) sultanas
200 g (7 oz) icing sugar

To decorate
several pieces of crystallized
    ginger, very thinly sliced

Line a 12-section bun tray with paper or foil cake cases. Peel and finely grate the ginger, working over a plate to catch the juice.

Put the butter, caster sugar, eggs, flour, baking powder and vanilla extract in a bowl. Add the grated ginger, reserving the juice for the icing. Beat with a hand-held electric whisk for about a minute until light and creamy. Stir in the sultanas and then divide the cake mixture between the cake cases.

Bake in a preheated oven, 180°C (350°F), Gas Mark 4, for 20 minutes or until risen and just firm to the touch. Transfer to a wire rack to cool.

Beat the icing sugar in a bowl with the ginger juice, making up with enough water to create an icing that just holds its shape. Spread over the tops of the cakes with a small palette knife. Decorate with the crystallized ginger slices.

Chocolate Orange Cupcakes

Makes 12
Preparation time 20 minutes,
plus cooling
Cooking time 25 minutes

125 g (4 oz) lightly salted
  butter, softened
125 g (4 oz) caster sugar
2 eggs
125 g (4 oz) self-raising flour
25 g (1 oz) cocoa powder
½ teaspoon baking powder
finely grated rind of 1 orange

Icing
100 g (3½ oz) plain chocolate,
  chopped
100 g (3½ oz) unsalted butter,
  softened
125 g (4 oz) icing sugar
2 tablespoons cocoa powder

To decorate
candied orange peel shavings
  (optional)

Line a 12-section bun tray with paper or foil cake cases. Put the lightly salted butter, caster sugar, eggs, flour, cocoa powder, baking powder and orange rind in a bowl and beat with a hand-held electric whisk for about a minute until light and creamy. Divide the cake mixture evenly between the cake cases.

Bake in a preheated oven, 180°C (350°F), Gas Mark 4, for 20 minutes or until risen and just firm to the touch. Transfer to a wire rack to cool.

To melt the chocolate, break into pieces and place in a heatproof bowl. Rest the bowl over a pan, one-third filled with water, making sure that the base of the bowl cannot come in contact with the water. Gently heat so the water is simmering. Don't stir the chocolate until it looks melted, then stir a couple of times until smooth. Overstirring will ruin the texture. It is crucial that no water, such as steam from the pan, gets into the bowl while the chocolate is melting, as this will make it solidify. Turn off the heat and leave to cool.

Beat together the unsalted butter, icing sugar and cocoa powder in a bowl until smooth and creamy. Stir in the melted chocolate. Pipe or swirl the icing over the tops of the cakes and decorate with candied orange peel shavings, if liked.

Rock Buns

Makes 20
Preparation time: 10 minutes
Cooking time: 15 minutes

125 g (4 oz) unsalted butter,
  softened
100 g (3½ oz) golden caster
  sugar
225 g (7½ oz) self-raising flour
1 teaspoon ground ginger
1 teaspoon ground cinnamon
1 egg, beaten
150 ml (¼ pint) milk
100 g (3½ oz) sultanas
75 g (3 oz) currants
50 g (2 oz) white sugar cubes

Grease 2 baking sheets. Cream together the butter and sugar until light and fluffy. Stir in the flour, spices, egg and milk and mix to a soft dough. Stir the dried fruits into the mixture.

Place dessertspoonfuls of the mixture on to the baking sheets, spacing them slightly apart.

Put the sugar cubes in a polythene bag and lightly crush with a rolling pin. Scatter over the buns and bake in a preheated oven, 190°C (375°F), Gas Mark 5, for about 15 minutes or until risen and golden. Transfer to a wire rack to cool.

Banana & Raisin Flapjacks

Makes 12
Preparation time 10 minutes
Cooking time 10 minutes

150 g (5 oz) butter
150 ml (¼ pint) maple syrup
125 g (4 oz) raisins
2 large bananas, well mashed
375 g (12 oz) porridge oats

Place the butter in a medium pan with the maple syrup and melt over a gentle heat. Stir in the raisins. Remove from the heat and add the bananas, stirring well. Add the oats and stir well until all the oats have been coated.

Spoon the mixture into a 28 x 18 cm (11 x 7 inch) nonstick Swiss roll tin and level the surface using a potato masher for ease. Bake in a preheated oven, 190°C (375°F), Gas Mark 5, for 10 minutes until the top is just beginning to turn a pale golden. The mixture will still seem somewhat soft.

Cool for 10 minutes in the tin before cutting into 12 squares. Remove from the tin and allow to cool completely.

Blondies

Makes 18
Preparation time: 15 minutes
Cooking time: 30–35 minutes

500 g (1 lb) white chocolate,
    broken into squares
75 g (3 oz) unsalted butter, cut
    into small pieces
3 eggs, lightly beaten
180 g (6 oz) caster sugar
180 g (6 oz) self-raising flour
180 g (6 oz) macadamia nuts,
    roughly chopped
1 teaspoon vanilla extract

Grease a 26 x 19 cm (11 x 7 inch) cake tin and line the base with nonstick baking paper.

Roughly chop 400 g (13 oz) of the chocolate and set aside. Melt the remaining chocolate and the butter together in a heat-proof bowl set over a pan of barely simmering water, stirring until smooth (see page 51). Remove the bowl from the heat and leave to cool slightly.

Beat the eggs and sugar together in a separate bowl, then gradually beat in the melted chocolate mixture. Sift the flour over the mixture and fold in together with the macadamia nuts, reserved chopped chocolate and the vanilla extract, mixing well.

Transfer the mixture to the prepared tin and level the surface. Bake in a preheated oven, 190°C (375°F), Gas Mark 5, for 30–35 minutes, or until the centre is only just firm to the touch. Remove from the oven and leave to cool completely in the tin. Cut into squares to serve.

Chocolate Mocha Brownies

Makes 15
Preparation time: 15 minutes
Cooking time: 30 minutes

200 g (7 oz) milk chocolate
250 g (8 oz) plain chocolate,
    broken into pieces
175 g (6 oz) unsalted butter
2 tablespoons instant coffee
3 eggs
225 g (7½ oz) light
    muscovado sugar
75 g (3 oz) self-raising flour
½ teaspoon baking powder

Grease and line a shallow 27 x 18 cm (11 x 7 inch) rectangular tin or a 23 cm (9 inch) square tin. Chop the milk chocolate into small chunks.

Melt the plain chocolate in a bowl with the butter, stirring frequently, until smooth. Stir in the coffee.

In a separate bowl beat together the eggs and sugar. Stir in the melted chocolate mixture. Sift the flour and baking powder into the bowl and stir until they are combined.

Add the chopped milk chocolate and turn the mixture into the tin. Level the surface and bake in a preheated oven, 190°C (375°F), Gas Mark 5, for about 30 minutes or until a crust has formed but the mixture feels quite soft underneath. Leave to cool in the tin, then serve cut into squares.

Chocolate Meringues

Makes 15
Preparation time 10 minutes
Cooking time 1½ hours

4 egg whites
250 g (8 oz) caster sugar
125 g (4 oz) plain dark chocolate, grated
284 ml (10 fl oz) double cream, whipped

Whisk the egg whites in a large clean bowl until stiff. Whisk in 1 tablespoon of the sugar, then fold in the rest with the grated chocolate.

Spoon or pipe 30 meringues onto 2 baking sheets lined with nonstick baking paper and bake in a preheated oven, 140°C (275°F), Gas Mark 1, for about 1½ hours or until dry and crisp. Peel the meringues off the paper and cool on a wire rack.

Sandwich the meringues together in pairs with the whipped cream.

Fresh Lemon Slices

Makes 36
Preparation time 15 minutes
Cooking time 38–42 minutes

250 g (8 oz) butter, softened
75 g (3 oz) icing sugar
1 teaspoon vanilla extract
250 g (8 oz) plain flour, sifted
4 eggs
175 g (6 oz) granulated sugar
grated rind of 1 lemon
6 tablespoons lemon juice

Put the butter, 50 g (2 oz) of the icing sugar and the vanilla extract into a mixing bowl and cream until light and fluffy. Fold the flour, a little at a time, into the creamed mixture until completely incorporated.

Generously grease a 30 x 23 cm (12 x 9 inch) shallow baking tin. Spread the mixture evenly in the prepared tin and bake in a preheated oven, 190°C (375°F), Gas Mark 5, for 20 minutes.

Meanwhile, put the eggs, granulated sugar, lemon rind and lemon juice into a bowl. Stir to blend the ingredients but do not beat. Pour the mixture over the baked pastry layer. Return the tin to the oven and bake for 18–22 minutes until the topping is set and lightly browned.

Remove the tin from the oven and sift the remaining icing sugar over the warm cake to cover generously. Cut the cake into slices. Remove from the tin when cool.

Madeleines

Makes 14
Preparation time 15 minutes
Cooking time 12 minutes

3 eggs
100 g (3½ oz) caster sugar
150 g (5 oz) plain flour
100 g (3½ oz) unsalted butter,
  melted
grated rind of 1 lemon
grated rind of 1 orange

Brush a tray of madeleine moulds with melted butter
and coat with plain flour, then tap the tray to remove the
excess flour.

Whisk the eggs and sugar in a bowl until thick and pale
and the whisk leaves a trail when lifted. Sift the flour, then
gently fold into the egg mixture. Fold in the melted butter
and lemon and orange rinds. Spoon into the moulds,
leaving a little room for rising.

Bake in a preheated oven, 200°C (400°F), Gas Mark 6,
for 12 minutes or until golden and springy to the touch.
Remove the madeleines from the tray and leave to cool
on a wire rack.

Everyday Cakes

Family Chocolate Cake

White Chocolate, Rum & Raisin Tea Bread

Banana Cake

Pear, Cardamom & Sultana Cake

Date & Walnut Loaf

Apple & Blackberry Crumble Cake

Victoria Sandwich Cake

Fruit Gingerbread

Cherry Cake

Spiced Marmalade Cake

Grandma's Courgette Loaf

Apricot Tea Bread

Lemon Drizzle Cake

Gooseberry & Elderflower Cake

Really Easy Fruitcake

Family Chocolate Cake

Serves 8
Preparation time 20 minutes,
  plus chilling
Cooking time 25 minutes

125 g (4 oz) caster sugar
4 eggs
100 g (3½ oz) self-raising flour
25 g (1 oz) cocoa powder
40 g (1½ oz) unsalted butter,
  melted
1 teaspoon vanilla extract

Icing
350 g (12 oz) dark chocolate
250 g (8 oz) unsalted butter
100 g (3½ oz) icing sugar,
  sifted

Put the sugar and eggs into a bowl set over a pan of gently simmering water and, using hand-held beaters, beat the mixture for 5 minutes or until it reaches the ribbon stage, or until the beaters leave a thick, ribbon-like trail when lifted from the batter.

Sift over the flour and cocoa powder and carefully fold into the mixture with the melted butter and vanilla extract until combined.

Oil and base-line a 20 cm (8 inch) spring-form cake tin. Pour the mixture into the tin and bake in a preheated oven, 180°C (350°F), Gas Mark 4, for 25 minutes until risen and firm to the touch. Remove from the oven and leave to cool in the tin for 5 minutes. Turn out and cool on a wire rack.

To make the icing, melt the chocolate and butter together in a bowl set over a pan of just simmering water (see page 51). Remove from the heat and beat in the icing sugar. Set aside to cool and then chill for 1 hour until thickened. Beat until pale and fluffy.

Cut the cake in half and use half the icing to sandwich the halves back together. Use the remaining icing to cover the top and sides of the cake, swirling the mixture with a palette knife.

White Chocolate, Rum & Raisin Tea Bread

Serves 8
Preparation time 10 minutes
Cooking time 40–45 minutes

100 g (3½ oz) white chocolate
125 g (4 oz) unsalted butter,
   softened
75 g (3 oz) golden caster
   sugar, plus extra for dusting
   (optional)
2 eggs
150 g (5 oz) self-raising flour
1 teaspoon baking powder
3 tablespoons white or
   dark rum
50 g (2 oz) raisins

Grease and line the base and sides of a 15 cm (6 inch) square tin or 500 g (1 lb) loaf tin. Grease the paper. Using a sharp knife, shave off a quarter of the chocolate into long shards. Roughly chop the rest.

Put the butter, sugar, eggs, flour, baking powder and rum in a bowl and beat together until smooth and creamy. Stir in the raisins and chopped chocolate and turn into the tin. Level the surface and scatter with the chocolate shards.

Bake in a preheated oven, 180°C (350°F), Gas Mark 4, for 40–45 minutes or until risen and golden and a skewer inserted into the centre comes out clean. Transfer to a wire rack to cool. Serve lightly dusted with caster sugar, if liked.

Banana Cake

Serves 6
Preparation time 15 minutes
Cooking time 20–25 minutes

125 g (4 oz) butter, softened
125 g (4 oz) caster sugar
2 eggs
125 g (4 oz) self-raising flour,
  sifted
icing sugar, to dust

Filling
50 g (2 oz) ground almonds
50 g (2 oz) icing sugar, sifted
1 small banana, mashed
½ teaspoon lemon juice

Cream the butter and sugar together in a mixing bowl until light and fluffy. Beat in the eggs, one at a time, adding a tablespoon of flour with the second egg. Fold in the remaining flour with the bananas.

Divide the mixture between two greased and lined 18 cm (7 inch) sandwich tins. Bake in a preheated oven, 180°C (350°F), Gas Mark 4, for 20–25 minutes or until the cakes spring back when lightly pressed. Turn out the cakes onto a wire rack to cool.

To make the filling, mix the ground almonds with the icing sugar, then add the banana and lemon juice and mix to a smooth paste. Sandwich the cakes together with the filling and dust the top of the cake with icing sugar.

Pear, Cardamom & Sultana Cake

Serves 12
Preparation time 20 minutes
Cooking time 1¼–1½ hours

125 g (4 oz) unsalted butter,
  softened
125 g (4 oz) light soft brown
  sugar
2 eggs, lightly beaten
250 g (8 oz) self-raising flour
1 teaspoon ground
  cardamom
4 tablespoons milk
500 g (1 lb) pears, peeled,
  cored and thinly sliced
125 g (4 oz) sultanas
1 tablespoon clear honey

Using electric beaters, cream the butter and sugar together until pale and light and then gradually beat in the eggs, a little at a time, until incorporated. Sift the flour and ground cardamom together and fold them into the creamed mixture with the milk.

Reserve about one-third of the pear slices and roughly chop the rest. Fold the chopped pears into the creamed mixture with the sultanas. Oil and base-line a 1 kg (2 lb) loaf tin with greaseproof paper and spoon the mixture into the tin. Smooth the surface, making a small dip in the centre.

Arrange the reserved pear slices down the centre of the cake, pressing them in gently. Bake in a preheated oven, 160°C (325°F), Gas Mark 3, for 1¼–1½ hours or until a skewer, inserted in the centre, comes out clean. Remove the cake from the oven and brush over the clear honey. Leave to cool in the tin for 20 minutes and then transfer to a wire rack to cool completely.

Date & Walnut Loaf

Serves 12
Preparation time 15 minutes
Cooking time 1–1¼ hours

125 g (4 oz) unsalted butter,
   cut into small pieces
125 g (4 oz) light muscovado
   sugar
50 g (2 oz) golden syrup
150 ml (¼ pint) milk
2 large eggs, beaten
250 g (8 oz) plain flour
1 level teaspoon bicarbonate
   of soda
1 teaspoon ground mixed
   spice
150 g (5 oz) stoned dried
   dates, chopped
50 g (2 oz) walnuts, chopped

Topping
50 g (2 oz) stoned dried
   dates, chopped
25 g (1 oz) walnuts, chopped
1 tablespoon caster sugar
1 teaspoon ground cinnamon

Grease and base-line a 900 g (2 lb) loaf tin.

Put the butter, sugar and golden syrup in a large saucepan and heat gently, stirring. When the butter has melted, remove the pan from the heat and set aside to cool for a few minutes.

Stir the milk and eggs into the cooled syrup mixture. Sift the flour, bicarbonate of soda and mixed spice into a bowl, then stir in the syrup mixture. Mix to a smooth batter, then fold in the dates and walnuts.

Pour the mixture evenly into the prepared tin. Mix the topping ingredients together and sprinkle thickly over the top of the cake.

Bake in a preheated oven, 150°C (300°F), Gas Mark 2, for 1–1¼ hours, or until a skewer inserted into the centre comes out clean. Cool in the tin for 5 minutes, then turn out onto a wire rack and leave to cool completely.

Apple & Blackberry Crumble Cake

Serves 16
Preparation time 30 minutes
Cooking time 45 minutes

175 g (6 oz) butter, softened
175 g (6 oz) caster sugar
3 eggs, beaten
200 g (7 oz) self-raising flour
1 teaspoon baking powder
grated rind of 1 lemon
500 g (1 lb) cooking apples,
    cored, peeled and thinly
    sliced
150 g (5 oz) frozen
    blackberries, just defrosted

Crumble topping

75 g (3 oz) self-raising flour
75 g (3 oz) muesli
50 g (2 oz) caster sugar
75 g (3 oz) butter, diced

Cream the butter and sugar together in a mixing bowl until pale and creamy. Gradually mix in alternate spoonfuls of beaten egg and flour until all has been added and the mixture is smooth. Stir in the baking powder and lemon rind then spoon the mixture into an 18 x 28 cm (7 x 11 inch) roasting tin lined with nonstick baking paper. Spread the surface level than arrange the apple slices and blackberries over the top.

To make the crumble topping, put the flour, muesli and caster sugar in a mixing bowl, add the butter and rub in with your fingertips until the mixture resembles fine breadcrumbs. Sprinkle over the top of the fruit. Bake in a preheated oven, 180°C (350°F), Gas Mark 4, for about 45 minutes until the crumble is golden brown and a skewer inserted into the centre comes out clean.

Leave to cool in the tin then lift out using the lining paper. Cut the cake into 16 bars and peel off the lining paper. Store in an airtight tin for up to 2 days.

Victoria Sandwich Cake

Serves 8
Preparation time 20 minutes
Cooking time 20 minutes

175 g (6 oz) butter, softened
175 g (6 oz) caster sugar
175 g (6 oz) brown rice flour
3 eggs
1 tablespoon baking powder
a few drops of vanilla essence
1 tablespoon milk

To decorate
4 tablespoons raspberry jam
sifted icing sugar, for dusting

Place all the cake ingredients in a mixing bowl or a food processor and beat well until smooth.

Divide the mixture evenly between 2 greased and floured 18 cm (7 inch) nonstick round cake tins and bake in a preheated oven, 200°C (400°F), Gas Mark 6, for about 20 minutes until golden and risen.

Remove from the oven and turn out on to a wire rack to cool. Sandwich the cakes together with the jam and dust with icing sugar.

Fruit Gingerbread

Serves 8
Preparation time 15 minutes
Cooking time 1–1¼ hours

400 g (13 oz) plain flour
1 teaspoon baking powder
1 tablespoon ground ginger
1 teaspoon ground cinnamon
225 g (7½ oz) unsalted butter,
   cut into small pieces
125 g (4 oz) molasses or black
   treacle
175 g (6 oz) soft light brown
   sugar
3 eggs, beaten
75 g (3 oz) dried cherries,
   halved
115 g (4 oz) stoned dried
   dates, chopped
50 g (2 oz) preserved stem
   ginger, drained and
   chopped
90 g (3½ oz) sultanas

Grease and base-line a deep 20cm (8 inch) square cake tin.

Mix the flour, baking powder and spices together in a large bowl. Set aside. Put the butter into a saucepan with the molasses or black treacle and sugar and stir over a low heat until melted. Pour into the flour mixture and mix well. Beat in the eggs until smooth, then stir in the dried cherries, dates, stem ginger and sultanas, mixing well.

Pour the mixture evenly into the prepared tin. Bake in a preheated oven, 150°C (300°F), Gas Mark 2, for 1–1¼ hours, or until a skewer inserted into the centre comes out clean. Cool in the tin for 10 minutes, then turn out onto a wire rack and leave to cool completely.

Cherry Cake

Serves 6
Preparation time 20 minutes
Cooking time 1½–2 hours

175 g (6 oz) butter, softened
175 g (6 oz) caster sugar
3 eggs
300 g (10 oz) self-raising flour, sifted
250 g (8 oz) glacé cherries, halved
50 g (2 oz) ground almonds
about 5 tablespoons milk

Cream the butter and the sugar together in a mixing bowl until light and fluffy. Beat in the eggs, one at a time, adding a tablespoon of flour with the last two.

Carefully fold in the remaining flour, then fold in the cherries, ground almonds and enough milk to give a dropping consistency.

Put the mixture into a greased and lined deep 18 cm (7 inch) cake tin and bake in a preheated oven, 160°C (325°F), Gas Mark 3, for 1½–2 hours. Leave the cake in the tin for 5 minutes, then turn on to a wire rack to cool.

Spiced Marmalade Cake

Serves 24
Preparation time 25 minutes
Cooking time 35–40 minutes

125 g (4 oz) butter
200 g (7 oz) golden syrup
100 g (3½ oz) caster sugar
2 tablespoons chunky
 marmalade
2 tablespoons chopped
 candied peel (optional)
250 g (8 oz) self-raising flour
2 teaspoons ground mixed
 spice
1 teaspoon ground ginger
½ teaspoon bicarbonate of
 soda
150 ml (¼ pint) milk
2 eggs, beaten

Topping
2 oranges, thinly sliced
50 g (2 oz) caster sugar
200 ml (7 fl oz) water
2 tablespoons marmalade

Put the butter, golden syrup, sugar and marmalade in a saucepan and heat gently until melted.

Remove from the heat and stir in the chopped peel, if using, and the dry ingredients. Add the milk and beaten eggs and mix until smooth. Pour into a 20 cm (8 inch) deep square cake tin, greased and base-lined with oiled greaseproof paper. Bake in a preheated oven, 180°C (350°F), Gas Mark 4, for 35–40 minutes until well risen and a skewer inserted into the centre comes out clean.

Meanwhile, put the sliced oranges into a saucepan with the sugar and water. Cover and simmer for 25 minutes until tender. Remove the lid and cook for 5 minutes more, until the liquid has been reduced to about 2 tablespoons. Add the marmalade and heat until melted.

Leave the cake to cool in the tin for 10 minutes then loosen the edges, turn out on to a wire rack and peel off the lining paper. Turn the cake the right way up and spoon over the oranges and sauce. Store in an airtight tin for up to 3 days.

Grandma's Courgette Loaf

Serves 8–10
Preparation time 30 minutes
Cooking time about 1 hour
   15 minutes

275 g (9 oz) self-raising flour
1 teaspoon baking powder
2 teaspoons mixed spice
2 courgettes, grated
125 g (4 oz) soft brown sugar
1 egg
75 ml (3 fl oz) milk
75 g (3 oz) butter, plus extra
   for greasing
75 g (3 oz) raisins
75 g (3 oz) walnuts, chopped

Topping
50 g (2 oz) plain flour
25 g (1 oz) soft brown sugar
½ teaspoon mixed spice
50 g (2 oz) chilled butter, cut
   into cubes
50 g (2 oz) walnuts, finely
   chopped

Grease a 1 kg (2 lb) loaf tin lightly with butter and line the base with nonstick baking paper. Sift the flour, baking powder and mixed spice into a large bowl and add the courgettes and sugar. Stir well.

Beat the egg and milk together in a jug. Melt the butter in a small pan, then add the raisins and stir well over a gentle heat for a few seconds to help plump them up. Pour the melted butter and milk and egg mixture into the dry ingredients and stir until well combined. Add the walnuts and stir again. Transfer to the prepared tin and level.

Make the streusel topping: mix the flour with the sugar and mixed spice, then rub the butter into the dry ingredients until the mixture resembles fine breadcrumbs. Stir in the walnuts, then scatter over the cake.

Bake the loaf in a preheated oven, 180°C (350°F), Gas Mark 4, for 1 hour to 1 hour 10 minutes until well risen and firm to the touch and a skewer inserted comes out clean. Allow it to cool for 10 minutes in the tin before turning out on to a wire rack to cool completely.

Apricot Tea Bread

Serves 10
Preparation time 25 minutes,
  plus soaking
Cooking time 1 hour

100 g (3½ oz) ready-to-eat
  dried apricots, chopped
100 g (3½ oz) sultanas
100 g (3½ oz) raisins
150 g (5 oz) caster sugar
300 ml (½ pint) hot strong tea
275 g (9 oz) self-raising flour
1 teaspoon bicarbonate of
  soda
1 teaspoon ground cinnamon
1 egg, beaten

Put the dried fruits and sugar in a mixing bowl, add the hot tea and mix together. Leave to soak for 4 hours or overnight.

Mix the flour, bicarbonate of soda and cinnamon together, add to the soaked fruit with the beaten egg and mix together well.

Spoon into a greased 1 kg (2 lb) loaf tin, its base and 2 long sides also lined with oiled greaseproof paper. Spread the surface level then bake in the centre of a preheated oven, 160°C (325°F), Gas Mark 3, for about 1 hour until well risen, the top has cracked and a skewer inserted into the centre comes out clean.

Leave to cool in the tin for 10 minutes then loosen the edges and lift out of the tin using the lining paper. Transfer to a wire rack, peel off the lining paper and leave to cool completely. Cut into slices and spread with a little butter to serve. Store, unbuttered, in an airtight tin for up to 1 week.

Lemon Drizzle Cake

Serves 8–10
Preparation time 20 minutes
Cooking time 50–60 minutes

225 g (7½ oz) unsalted butter, softened
225 g (7½ oz) caster sugar
finely grated rind of 3 lemons, plus 100 ml (3½ fl oz) lemon juice
4 eggs, beaten
250 g (8 oz) self-raising flour
1 teaspoon baking powder
75 g (3 oz) ground almonds
100 g (3½ oz) granulated sugar

Grease and line the base and sides of a 20 cm (8 inch) round cake tin or an 18 cm (7 inch) square tin. Grease the paper. Cream together the butter, caster sugar and the lemon rind until light and fluffy.

Beat in the eggs, a little at a time, beating well between each addition. Add a little of the flour if the mixture starts to curdle. Sift the flour and baking powder into the bowl, add the ground almonds and 2 tablespoons of the lemon juice and gently fold in using a large metal spoon.

Turn the mixture into the tin and level the surface. Bake in a preheated oven, 180°C (350°F), Gas Mark 4, for about 45 minutes or until just firm and a skewer inserted into the centre comes out clean.

Meanwhile, mix together the remaining lemon juice with the granulated sugar. Transfer the cake to a wire rack. Give the lemon mixture a good stir and spoon it over the cake. As the cake cools the syrup will sink into the cake, leaving a sugary crust.

Gooseberry & Elderflower Cake

Serves 8
Preparation time 15 minutes
Cooking time 45 minutes

280 g (9 oz) self-raising flour
1 teaspoon baking powder
100 g (3½ oz) caster sugar
125 g (4 oz) soft light brown
   sugar
125 g (4 oz) unsalted butter,
   melted
2 eggs, beaten
350 g (11½ oz) cooked
   unsweetened gooseberries
2 tablespoons elderflower
   cordial

Icing

125 g (4 oz) icing sugar, sifted
3–5 teaspoons elderflower
   cordial

Grease and base-line a 23 cm (9 inch) springform tin fitted with a flat base.

Mix the flour, baking powder and sugars together in a bowl. Add the melted butter and eggs and mix well. Stir in the gooseberries and elderflower cordial until well combined. Spoon the mixture into the prepared tin and level the surface.

Bake in a preheated oven, 180°C (350°F), Gas Mark 4, for about 45 minutes, or until a skewer inserted into the centre comes out clean. Cool in the tin for 5 minutes, then turn out onto a wire rack and leave to cool completely.

When the cake is cold, make the icing. Put the icing sugar in a bowl and stir in just enough elderflower cordial to make a thick pouring consistency. Using a teaspoon, drizzle the icing randomly and decoratively over the top of the cake. Leave to set.

Really Easy Fruit Cake

Serves 8
Preparation time 20 minutes
Cooking time 1–1¼ hours

250 g (8 oz) self-raising flour
½ teaspoon ground mixed
   spice
½ teaspoon ground cinnamon
125 g (4 oz) butter or
   margarine
125 g (4 oz) soft brown sugar
125 g (4 oz) currants
50 g (2 oz) glacé cherries,
   quartered
1 large egg
75 ml (3 fl oz) milk
demerara sugar, for sprinkling
   (optional)

Mix together the flour, mixed spice and cinnamon in a large bowl. Add the butter and rub in with your fingertips until the mixture resembles breadcrumbs. Stir in the sugar, currants and glacé cherries.

Whisk together the egg and milk in a separate bowl, add to the fruit mixture and beat thoroughly.

Pour the mixture into a greased 20 cm (8 inch) square cake tin lined with nonstick baking paper. Sprinkle the top with a little demerara sugar, if liked. Bake in a preheated oven, 180°C (350°F), Gas Mark 4, for 1–1¼ hours until the top is firm but springy to the touch; a skewer inserted into the centre of the cake should come out clean. Leave to stand in the tin for a few minutes, then turn out on to a wire rack to cool completely. Cut into squares to serve.

Special Occasion Cakes

Summer Berry Sponge
Chocolate Fudge Ring
Very Rich Chocolate Gateau
Carrot & Walnut Cake
St Clements Cake
Rum & Raisin Cheesecake
Chocolate Cheesecake
Hazelnut Meringue Gateau
Peach & Redcurrant Cream Sponge
Banana Cream Roll
Date Chocolate Torte
Chocolate & Chestnut Roulade

Summer Berry Sponge

Serves 6–8
Preparation time 30 minutes,
    plus cooling
Cooking time 10–12 minutes

4 eggs
100 g (3½ oz) caster sugar
100 g (3½ oz) plain flour
finely grated rind and
    2 tablespoons juice of
    1 lemon
150 ml (¼ pint) double cream
150 g (5 oz) fromage frais
3 tablespoons lemon curd
500 g (1 lb) small strawberries,
    halved
150 g (5 oz) blueberries
4 tablespoons redcurrant jelly
1 tablespoon water (or lemon
    juice)

Whisk the eggs and caster sugar in a large bowl until very thick and the mixture leaves a trail when lifted. Sift the flour over the surface of the eggs, then fold in very gently. Add the lemon rind and juice and fold in until just mixed. Pour the mixture into a greased, floured 25 cm (10 inch) sponge flan tin, tilting the tin to ease into an even layer.

Bake in a preheated oven, 180°C (350°F), Gas Mark 4, for 10–12 minutes until the top of the sponge is golden and the centre springs back when lightly pressed. Cool the sponge in the tin for 5–10 minutes, then carefully turn it out on to a wire rack to cool.

Whip the cream until it forms soft swirls, then fold in the fromage frais and lemon curd. Transfer the sponge to a serving plate, spoon the cream into the centre, spread into an even layer, then top with the strawberries and blueberries. Warm the redcurrant jelly in a small saucepan with the measured water (or lemon juice), then brush over the fruit.

Chocolate Fudge Ring

Serves 12
Preparation time 20 minutes,
    plus cooling
Cooking time 40 minutes

175 g (6 oz) self-raising flour
50 g (2 oz) cocoa powder
2 teaspoons baking powder
175 g (6 oz) caster sugar
175 g (6 oz) butter
4 eggs
2 teaspoons vanilla essence
4 tablespoons milk

Icing
300 g (10 oz) plain dark
    chocolate, broken into
    pieces
4 tablespoons milk
50 g (2 oz) butter
225 g (7½ oz) icing sugar, plus
    extra for dusting

To decorate
walnut halves

Sift the flour, cocoa powder and baking powder into a bowl. Add the sugar, butter, eggs, vanilla essence and milk and whisk until they are evenly combined.

Grease and line the base of a 1.8 litre (3 pint) ring cake tin. Turn the mixture into the tin and level the surface. Bake in a preheated oven, 180°C (350°F), Gas Mark 4, for 35 minutes or until just firm to the touch. Use a palette knife to loosen the cake from the side of the tin, then invert the cake on to a wire rack and leave to cool.

Heat the chocolate gently in a heavy-based pan with the milk until it has melted, stirring frequently. Stir in the butter. Beat in the icing sugar and leave the mixture to cool slightly.

Split the cake horizontally into 3 layers. Beat the icing again until it has a slightly fudge-like texture. Use a little icing to sandwich the layers together. Spread the remaining icing over the top and sides of the cake, swirling it with a palette knife. Decorate the top of the cake with the walnut halves and dust with icing sugar.

Very Rich Chocolate Gateau

Serves 12–14
Preparation time 25 minutes,
   plus cooling and setting
Cooking time 40 minutes

200 g (7 oz) plain dark
   chocolate
2 tablespoons milk
175 g (6 oz) butter
175 g (6 oz) caster sugar
175 g (6 oz) ground hazelnuts
   or almonds
40 g (1½ oz) plain flour
5 eggs, separated
3 tablespoons hot water

Syrup
25 g (1 oz) caster sugar
4 tablespoons brandy or
   orange/coffee liqueur
50 ml (2 fl oz) water

Glaze
5 tablespoons apricot jam
25 g (1 oz) caster sugar
75 ml (3 fl oz) water
200 g (7 oz) plain dark
   chocolate
25 g (1 oz) milk chocolate

Melt 200 g (7 oz) plain dark chocolate with the milk in a bowl over a pan of simmering water (see page 51). Put the chocolate mixture, butter, 175 g (6 oz) sugar, hazelnuts or almonds, flour and egg yolks in a bowl with the measured hot water and beat until smooth.

Whisk the egg whites until peaking, then fold them into the chocolate mixture.

Grease and line a 23 cm (9 inch) cake tin. Turn the mixture into the tin and level. Bake in a preheated oven, 180°C (350°F), Gas Mark 4, for about 30 minutes until just firm. Cover with a damp tea towel and leave to cool.

Mix 25 g (1 oz) sugar, the brandy or liqueur and measured water in a small pan and heat gently until the sugar dissolves. Boil rapidly for 1 minute until syrupy. Invert the cake on to a wire rack, remove the lining paper and spoon the syrup over the top.

Heat the apricot jam, press through a sieve and brush over the cake.

Heat 25 g (1 oz) caster sugar in a small, heavy-based pan with 75 ml (3 fl oz) water until the sugar has dissolved. Boil rapidly for 1 minute. Remove from the heat, leave for 1 minute, then stir in 200 g (7 oz) plain dark chocolate. Stir frequently until melted. Leave until beginning to thicken. Melt the milk chocolate.

Pour the chocolate glaze over the cake, easing it down the side with a palette knife. Drizzle the milk chocolate around the top edges of the cake to give a decorative finish. Leave in a cool place to set.

Carrot & Walnut Cake

Serves 10
Preparation time 40 minutes
Cooking time 25 minutes

150 ml (¼ pint) sunflower oil
3 eggs
175 g (6 oz) light muscovado
  sugar
175 g (6 oz) self-raising flour
1½ teaspoons baking powder
grated rind of ½ orange
1 teaspoon ground cinnamon
150 g (5 oz) carrots, coarsely
  grated
50 g (2 oz) walnuts, finely
  chopped

Maple frosting
250 ml (8 fl oz) maple syrup
2 egg whites
pinch of salt

To decorate
5 walnut halves, halved

Put the oil, eggs and sugar in a mixing bowl and whisk together until smooth.

Add the flour, baking powder, orange rind and ground cinnamon and whisk again until smooth. Stir in the grated carrots and chopped nuts. Divide the mixture between 2 x 20 cm (8 inch) sandwich tins, greased and base-lined with oiled greaseproof paper, and level.

Bake in a preheated oven, 180°C (350°F), Gas Mark 4, for about 20 minutes until the tops spring back when pressed. Cool for 5 minutes, then turn out on to a wire rack and peel off the lining paper. Leave to cool.

Make the maple frosting. Pour the maple syrup into a saucepan and heat to 115°C (240°F) on a sugar thermometer. As the temperature begins to rise, whisk the egg whites and salt in a clean bowl until stiff. When the syrup is ready, whisk it into the egg whites in a thin trickle until the frosting is like a meringue mixture. Keep whisking for a few minutes more until very thick.

Cut each cake in half then sandwich 4 layers together with frosting. Transfer to a serving plate, then swirl the rest of the frosting over the top and sides of the cake. Decorate the top with the walnut pieces.

St Clements Cake

Serves 8
Preparation time 30 minutes
Cooking time 20 minutes

175 g (6 oz) soft margarine
175 g (6 oz) caster sugar
175 g (6 oz) self-raising flour
1 teaspoon baking powder
3 eggs
finely grated rind of 1 lemon
finely grated rind of 1 orange
sifted icing sugar, for dusting

Filling
3 tablespoons lemon curd
150 ml (¼ pint) double cream,
  whipped

Beat all of the cake ingredients in a mixing bowl or a food processor until smooth.

Spoon the cake mixture evenly into 2 greased and base-lined 18 cm (7 inch) sandwich tins and spread the surfaces level. Bake in a preheated oven, 180°C (350°F), Gas Mark 4, for 20 minutes until well risen, the cakes are golden brown and spring back when gently pressed with a fingertip.

Leave to cool in the tin for 5 minutes then loosen the edges, turn out on to a wire rack and peel off the lining paper. Leave to cool.

Transfer one of the cakes to a serving plate and spread with the lemon curd. Spoon the whipped cream on top then cover with the remaining cake. Dust the top of the cake lightly with sifted icing sugar. This is best eaten on the day it is made.

Rum & Raisin Cheesecake

Serves 8
Preparation time 20 minutes,
  plus soaking and chilling
Cooking time 1 hour
  5 minutes–1¼ hours

4 eggs
4 tablespoons caster sugar
finely grated rind and juice
  of 1 lemon
227 g (8 oz) cottage cheese,
  sieved
284 ml (10 fl oz) soured cream
1 tablespoon plain flour
100 g (3½ oz) raisins, soaked
  overnight in 2 tablespoons
  rum
sifted icing sugar, to dust

Pastry
175 g (6 oz) plain flour
pinch of salt
1 tablespoon icing sugar
125 g (4 oz) butter
1 tablespoon iced water

Sift the flour, salt and icing sugar together into a mixing bowl. Rub in the butter until the mixture resembles coarse crumbs, then stir in the water. Gather the dough together and press it into the base and sides of a 23 cm (9 inch) loose-bottomed flan tin. Chill for 1 hour.

Line the pastry case with greaseproof or nonstick baking paper, add a layer of baking beans and blind bake in a preheated oven 180˚C (350˚F), Gas Mark 4 for 15 minutes or until firm. Carefully remove the greaseproof or baking paper and beans and bake for a further 5 minutes.

To make the filling, beat together the eggs and sugar in a mixing bowl, then add the remaining ingredients and stir well. Pour into the pastry case and return to the oven or 45–50 minutes. Turn off the heat and leave in the oven until completely cool. Sprinkle generously with icing sugar to serve.

Chocolate Cheesecake

Serves 14
Preparation time 45 minutes,
** plus cooling and chilling**
Cooking time 50 minutes

225 g (7½ oz) digestive
  biscuits, broken into crumbs
65 g (2½ oz) butter, melted
225 g (7½ oz) plain dark
  chocolate
225 g (7½ oz) white chocolate
350 g (11½ oz) cream cheese
500 g (1 lb) fromage frais
175 g (6 oz) golden caster
  sugar
3 eggs

Grease and line the base of a 23 cm (9 inch) springform tin. Mix the biscuit crumbs with the melted butter and press into the base of the prepared tin. Melt the plain dark and white chocolate in separate bowls over pans of simmering water (see page 51).

Whiz the cream cheese, fromage frais, sugar and eggs in a food processor until smooth. Tip half the mix into the melted plain dark chocolate, and the other half into the melted white chocolate, and stir until smooth. Spoon half the white chocolate mix over the biscuit base, top with the dark chocolate mix, then finish with the rest of the white chocolate mix. Drag a skewer through the white and dark layers to marble the top.

Bake in a preheated oven, 160°C (325°F), Gas Mark 3, for 50 minutes until slightly risen and just firm to the touch. Leave to cool, then chill.

Hazelnut Meringue Gateau

Serves 8–10
Preparation time 30 minutes,
 plus cooling and chilling
Cooking time 1–1¼ hours

5 eggs, separated
300 g (10 oz) caster sugar
1 tablespoon cornflour
125 g (4 oz) blanched
 hazelnuts, toasted and
 finely ground
250 g (8 oz) plain dark
 chocolate, broken into
 pieces
200 ml (7 fl oz) double cream
cocoa powder, for dusting

Chocolate hazelnuts
50 g (2 oz) plain dark
 chocolate, broken into
 pieces
50 g (2 oz) hazelnuts

Line 3 baking sheets and draw a 23 cm (9 inch) circle on each piece of baking paper.

Whisk the egg whites until stiff, then gradually whisk in the sugar until thick and glossy. Fold in the cornflour and ground hazelnuts until evenly incorporated and transfer the mixture to a large piping bag fitted with a 1 cm (½ inch) plain nozzle. Starting in the centre of each prepared circle, pipe the mixture in a continuous coil, finishing just within the marked line.

Bake in a preheated oven, 150°C (300°F), Gas Mark 2, for 1–1¼ hours until lightly golden and dried out. Remove from the oven and transfer to a wire rack to cool completely. Peel away the baking paper.

Melt the chocolate (see page 51) together with the cream over a pan of gently simmering water to make the filling. Cool, then chill for 1 hour until thickened.

Melt the chocolate for the chocolate hazelnuts and use a fork to dip in the hazelnuts until coated. Leave to set on baking paper.

Beat the chocolate filling until it is light and fluffy and use to sandwich the meringue layers together. Decorate the gateau with the chocolate hazelnuts and serve dusted with sifted cocoa powder.

Peach & Redcurrant Cream Sponge

Serves 8–10
Preparation time 20 minutes
Cooking time 20–25 minutes

100 g (3½ oz) caster sugar
4 eggs
100 g (3½ oz) plain flour

Filling
100 g (3½ oz) redcurrants
150 ml (¼ pint) double or
    whipping cream
1 tablespoon caster sugar,
    plus extra for dusting
1 ripe, juicy peach, sliced

Grease and base-line 2 x 20 cm (8 inch) sandwich tins.

Put the sugar and eggs in a large heatproof bowl over a pan of hot water and whisk for 6–8 minutes or until the whisk leaves a trail when lifted from the bowl. Remove from the heat and whisk for a further 2 minutes.

Sift half the flour into the bowl and fold in using a large metal spoon. Sift and fold in the remaining flour.

Turn the mixture into the tins and spread gently to the edges. Bake in a preheated oven, 190°C (375°F), Gas Mark 5, for 20–25 minutes or until just firm to the touch. Transfer to a wire rack to cool.

Reserve a few redcurrant sprigs. Remove the berries of the remainder by running the stalks between the tines of a fork. Whip the cream with 1 tablespoon sugar and spread it over one cake layer. Scatter with the fruits and place the second cake on top. Decorate with the reserved sprigs and dust with a little more sugar.

Banana Cream Roll

Serves 8
Preparation time 25 minutes
Cooking time 15 minutes

3 eggs, separated
2 teaspoons water
175 g (6 oz) caster sugar
125 g (4 oz) self-raising flour,
   sifted
pinch of salt
125 g (4 oz) walnut pieces,
   ground
granulated sugar, for dusting

Filling
3 bananas
1 tablespoon lemon juice
284 ml (10 fl oz) double
   cream, whipped
icing sugar, to taste
walnut halves, to decorate

Whisk the egg whites and water together in a large clean bowl until firm. Add the caster sugar, a tablespoon at a time, and continue to whisk until stiff. Lightly beat the egg yolks and fold into the mixture. Fold the flour, salt and walnuts into the egg mixture. Turn into a lined and greased 20 x 30 cm (8 x 12 inch) Swiss roll tin and bake in a preheated oven, 200°C (400°F), Gas Mark 6, for 15 minutes or until firm to the touch.

Sprinkle a sheet of greaseproof paper with granulated sugar. Turn the sponge onto the greaseproof paper and remove the lining paper. Trim the edges of the sponge and gently roll up with the greaseproof paper inside. Leave to cool.

Mash the bananas with the lemon juice, fold into just over half the cream and add icing sugar to taste.

Unroll the sponge carefully, remove the greaseproof paper and spread the sponge with banana filling. Re-roll and place on a serving dish. Pipe the remaining cream along the top and decorate with the walnuts.

Date Chocolate Torte

Serves 6–8
Preparation time 10 minutes,
    plus cooling
Cooking time 30 minutes

100 g (3½ oz) flaked almonds
125 g (4 oz) plain dark
    chocolate, roughly chopped
125 g (4 oz) dried ready-to-
    eat dates, pitted
3 egg whites
125 g (4 oz) caster sugar,
    plus 2 tablespoons for the
    topping
125 ml (4 fl oz) whipping
    cream
cocoa powder, to sprinkle

Grease a 23 cm (9 inch) springform tin and line with nonstick baking paper. Put the almonds and chocolate in a food processor and pulse until finely chopped. Finely chop the dates with a knife.

Whisk the egg whites in a large, perfectly clean bowl until soft peaks form. Slowly add the 125 g (4 oz) sugar and continue whisking until it has dissolved. Fold in the almond and chocolate mixture, then the dates. Spoon the mixture into the prepared tin and level the surface.

Bake in a preheated oven, 180°C (350°F), Gas Mark 4, for 30 minutes or until set and starting to come away from the side. Leave to cool in the tin before carefully turning out on to a serving plate.

Whip the cream and the remaining 2 tablespoons sugar in a small bowl until soft peaks form. Using a spatula, spread the cream evenly over the top of the torte. Serve cut into thin slices and dusted with cocoa.

Choc & Chestnut Roulade

Serves 8
Preparation time 20 minutes,
  plus cooling
Cooking time 25 minutes

125 g (4 oz) plain dark
  chocolate, broken into
  pieces
5 eggs, separated
175 g (6 oz) caster sugar,
  plus extra to sprinkle
2 tablespoons cocoa powder,
  sifted
250 g (8 oz) canned
  unsweetened chestnut
  purée
4 tablespoons icing sugar
1 tablespoon brandy
250 ml (8 fl oz) double cream
icing sugar, for dusting

Melt the chocolate (see page 51), then leave to cool for
5 minutes. Put the egg yolks in a bowl, add the sugar and
whisk together for 5 minutes until pale and thickened.
Stir in the melted chocolate and cocoa. Whisk the egg
whites in a clean bowl until stiff and fold into the chocolate
mixture until evenly combined.

Grease and line a 33 x 23 cm (13 x 9 inch) Swiss roll tin.
Transfer the mixture to the tin, spreading it well into
the corners, and smooth the surface with a palette knife.
Bake in a preheated oven, 180°C (350°F), Gas Mark 4, for
20 minutes until risen and set.

Sprinkle a large sheet of baking paper with caster sugar.
Remove the roulade from the oven and turn it out
immediately on to the sugared paper. Carefully remove the
lining paper and cover the roulade with a clean tea towel.
Set aside to cool.

Put the chestnut purée and icing sugar in a food processor
and purée until smooth (or combine well by hand).
Transfer the mixture to a bowl and stir in the brandy.
Gently whisk in the cream until light and fluffy. Spread the
filling over the roulade, leaving a 1 cm (½ inch) border,
and roll it up from one short end to form a log. Serve
dusted with sifted icing sugar.

Pies & Tarts

End-of-Summer Custard Pie
Deep Dish Puff Apple Pie
Mixed Berry Pies
Apricot Jam Tart
Treacle Tart
Cherry Frangipane Tart
Classic Lemon Tart
Custard Tart
Double Chocolate tart
French Onion Tarts
Sausage Slice
Venison & Red Wine Pie
Chicken & Mushroom Pies
Cockle, Leek & Bacon Pies

End-of-Summer Custard Pie

Serves 6–8
Preparation time 20 minutes, plus chilling
Cooking time 25 minutes

150 g (5 oz) plain flour, plus extra for dusting
3 tablespoons custard powder
2 tablespoons icing sugar
75 g (3 oz) butter, chilled and cut into cubes
2–3 tablespoons cold water
500 g (1 lb) blackberries
2 apples, peeled, cored and roughly chopped
4 tablespoons caster sugar
1 tablespoon clear honey
beaten egg

Sift the flour, custard powder and icing sugar into a bowl. Rub the butter using your fingertips into the flour until the mixture resembles fine breadcrumbs. Sprinkle over the measured water, then using a round-bladed knife begin to work the mixture into a smooth, firm dough. Wrap and chill for 15 minutes.

Toss the blackberries and apples with the sugar and honey and place in a 20 cm (8 inch) round pie dish or ovenproof dish.

Roll out the pastry, on a well-floured surface, to a round slightly larger than the pie dish. Place the dish on the pastry and cut around it using a sharp knife to produce a circle the correct size for the top. Using the pastry trimmings, make a border strip about 1 cm (½ inch) wide. Dampen the edges of the pie dish and fit the strips of pastry around the edge, pressing firmly. Dampen this pastry too before placing the circle on top and pressing again firmly to hold in place. Using any remaining trimmings, decorate the pie with leaves, flowers, birds or other shapes.

Brush with beaten egg to glaze and bake in a preheated oven, 200°C (400°F), Gas Mark 6, for 20–25 minutes until golden and crisp. Serve with vanilla ice cream or crème fraîche, if liked.

Deep Dish Puff Apple Pie

Serves 6
Preparation time 40 minutes
Cooking time 20–25 minutes

1 kg (2 lb) or about 5 cooking
   apples, quartered, cored,
   peeled and thickly sliced
100 g (3½ oz) caster sugar,
   plus extra for sprinkling
grated rind of 1 small orange
½ teaspoon ground mixed
   spice or ground cinnamon
3 whole cloves
400 g (13 oz) chilled
   ready-made puff pastry
beaten egg, to glaze

Fill a 1.2 litre (2 pint) pie dish with the apples. Mix the sugar with the orange rind, mixed spice or cinnamon and cloves, then sprinkle over the apples.

Roll the pastry out on a lightly floured surface until a little larger than the top of the dish. Cut 2 long strips from the edges, about 1 cm (½ inch) wide. Brush the dish rim with a little beaten egg, press the strips on top, then brush these with egg. Lift the remaining pastry over the dish and press the edges together well.

Trim off the excess pastry. Press your first and second finger on to the pie edge, then make small cuts between them with a small knife to create a scalloped edge. Repeat all the way around the pie. Reroll the trimmings and cut out small heart shapes or circles with a small biscuit cutter. Brush the top of the pie with beaten egg, add the pastry shapes, then brush these with egg. Sprinkle with a little extra sugar.

Bake in a preheated oven, 200°C (400°F), Gas Mark 6, for 20–25 minutes until the pastry is well risen and golden. Serve pie warm with spoonfuls of crème fraîche or extra-thick cream.

Mixed Berry Pies

Makes 12
Preparation time 40 minutes
Cooking time 30–35 minutes

400 g (13 oz) mixed
  redcurrants and
  blackcurrants or all
  blackcurrants
2 tablespoons water
150 g (5 oz) caster sugar,
  plus extra for sprinkling
1 tablespoon cornflour
175 g (6 oz) raspberries
200 g (7 oz) small
  strawberries, quartered
1½ quantities all-butter
  sweet shortcrust pastry
  (see page 9)
milk, to glaze

Cook the currants with the measurement water and sugar in a saucepan for 5 minutes, stirring until soft. Mix the cornflour with a little extra water until a smooth paste, then stir into the fruit and cook until thickened. Add the raspberries and strawberries, stir gently together, then leave to cool.

Reserve one-third of the pastry, then roll out the remainder thinly on a lightly floured surface. Stamp out 12 × 10 cm (4 inch) circles with a fluted biscuit cutter and press into a buttered 12-section muffin tin. Reknead and reroll the pastry trimmings as needed.

Spoon the fruit into the pies. Roll out the reserved pastry and any pastry trimmings and cut out 12 × 7 cm (3 inch) lids with a fluted biscuit cutter. Cut a small flower, heart or star in the centre of each. Brush the top edges of the fruit-filled pies with a little milk, add the pastry lids and press the edges together well to seal.

Brush the pies with a little milk and sprinkle with sugar. Bake in a preheated oven, 180°C (350°F), Gas Mark 4, for 25–30 minutes until golden. Leave to stand in the tins for 20 minutes, then loosen the edges with a knife and lift out of the tins. Serve warm with cream.

Apricot Jam Tart

Serves 6–8
Preparation time 20 minutes,
   plus chilling
Cooking time 20–25 minutes

275 g (9 oz) plain flour, plus
   extra for dusting
75 g (3 oz) caster sugar
125 g (4 oz) unsalted butter,
   diced
1 egg plus 1 egg yolk, lightly
   beaten
250 g (8 oz) apricot jam
icing sugar, for dusting

Put the flour and caster sugar in a bowl, add the butter and rub in with your fingertips until the mixture resembles coarse breadcrumbs. Gradually mix in enough of the eggs to bring the pastry together. Knead very lightly into a dough. Cover with clingfilm and chill for 30–45 minutes.

Roll two-thirds of the pastry out on a lightly floured work surface. Use to line a shallow, 23 cm (9 inch) fluted tart tin, then fill with the jam. Roll the remaining pastry out to a thickness of about 5 mm (¼ inch), then cut strips about 1 cm (½ inch) wide. Lightly brush the rim of the pastry case with water. Arrange the pastry strips in a lattice pattern over the tart. Chill for 20 minutes until firm.

Bake on a baking sheet in a preheated oven, 200°C (400°F), Gas Mark 6, for 20–25 minutes until the pastry is firm and golden. Leave to cool on a wire rack, then remove from the tin and serve with a generous dusting of icing sugar. The tart will keep in an airtight container for up to 2 days.

Treacle Tart

Serves 4–6
Preparation time 20 minutes, plus chilling
Cooking time 30–35 minutes

250 g (8 oz) golden syrup
75 g (3 oz) fresh white breadcrumbs
grated rind of ½ lemon

Pastry
175 g (6 oz) plain flour
75 g (3 oz) butter, diced
1–2 tablespoons iced water

Sift the flour into a bowl, then rub in the butter with your fingertips until the mixture resembles fine breadcrumbs. Add the iced water gradually and mix to a firm dough.

Turn out onto a lightly floured surface and knead lightly. Roll out thinly to a 23 cm (9 inch) circle. Use to line an 18 cm (7 inch) flan tin placed on a baking sheet. Chill the tart case and pastry trimmings in the refrigerator for 15 minutes.

Mix the syrup, bread crumbs and lemon rind together and spread over the pastry. Roll out the pastry trimmings, cut into long narrow strips and use to make a lattice pattern over the top of the filling.

Bake the tart in a preheated oven, 200°C (400°F), Gas Mark 6, for about 30–35 minutes until golden. Serve warm with cream.

Cherry Frangipane Tart

Serves 8
Preparation time 35 minutes,
  plus chilling
Cooking time 50 minutes

450 g (14½ oz) chilled
  ready-made or homemade
  sweet shortcrust pastry
  (see page 9)
250 g (8 oz) fresh cherries,
  pitted, or a 425 g (14 oz)
  can, drained
3 eggs
100 g (3½ oz) caster sugar
75 g (3 oz) unsalted butter,
  melted
few drops of almond essence
100 g (3½ oz) ground almonds
2 tablespoons flaked almonds
sifted icing sugar, for dusting

Roll out the pastry on a lightly floured surface until large enough to line a buttered 25 cm (10 inch) deep-fluted, loose-bottomed tart tin. Lift the pastry over a rolling pin, drape into the tin and press it over the base and sides. Trim off excess pastry with scissors so that it stands a little above the top of the tin. Prick the base of the tart with a fork, then chill for 15 minutes.

Line the pastry with nonstick baking paper, add baking beans and bake blind in a preheated oven, 190°C (375°F), Gas Mark 5, for 15 minutes. Remove the paper and beans and cook for a further 5 minutes. Reduce the oven temperature to 180°C (350°F), Gas Mark 4.

Arrange the cherries in the base of the tart. Whisk the eggs and sugar together until thick and the whisk leaves a trail when lifted out of the mixture. Gently fold in the melted butter and almond essence, then the ground almonds. Pour the mixture over the cherries and sprinkle with the flaked almonds.

Cook the tart for 30 minutes until golden brown and the filling is set. Check after 20 minutes and cover the top loosely with foil if the tart seems to be browning too quickly.

Leave to cool in the tin for 30 minutes, then remove and dust with sifted icing sugar before serving.

Classic Lemon Tart

Serves 8
Preparation time 20 minutes,
　plus chilling
Cooking time 40–45 minutes

3 eggs
1 egg yolk
475 ml (16 fl oz) double cream
100 g (3½ oz) sugar
150 ml (¼ pint) lemon juice

Pastry
200 g (7 oz) plain flour
½ teaspoon salt
100 g (3½ oz) butter, diced
2 tablespoons icing sugar,
　plus extra for dusting
2 egg yolks
1–2 teaspoons cold water

To make the pastry, put the flour and salt in a mixing bowl, add the butter and rub in with your fingertips or using an electric mixer until you have fine crumbs.

Stir in the icing sugar and gradually work in the egg yolks and the measurement water to form a firm dough. Knead the dough briefly on a lightly floured surface, then wrap with clingfilm and chill for 30 minutes. Roll out the dough and use to line a 25 cm (10 inch) fluted pie dish or tart tin. Prick the pastry case with a fork and chill for 20 minutes.

Line the pastry case with nonstick baking paper and baking beans and blind bake in a preheated oven, 200°C (400°F), Gas Mark 6, for 10 minutes. Remove the paper and beans and bake for a further 10 minutes until crisp and golden. Remove from the oven and reduce the oven temperature to 150°C (300°F), Gas Mark 2.

Beat together all the filling ingredients, pour them into the pastry case and bake for 20–25 minutes, or until the filling is just set. Let the tart cool completely, dust with sifted icing sugar and serve.

Custard Tart

Serves 6
Preparation time 20 minutes, plus chilling
Cooking time 1¼–1½ hours

250 g (8 oz) sweet shortcrust pastry (see page 9)
4 eggs
25 g (1 oz) caster sugar
½ teaspoon vanilla extract
1 teaspoon grated nutmeg

Roll out the pastry on a lightly floured surface and use to line a 20 cm (8 inch) flan tin. Chill in the refrigerator for 30 minutes.

Line the pastry case with greaseproof or nonstick baking paper, add a layer of baking beans and blind bake in a preheated oven, 200°C (400°F), Gas Mark 6, for 15 minutes. Remove the paper and beans and then return the pastry case to the oven for 5 minutes.

Lightly beat the eggs with the sugar and vanilla extract in a mixing bowl. Heat the milk in a saucepan until warm and whisk in the egg mixture. Strain into the cooked tart case and sprinkle with nutmeg. Bake the tart in a preheated oven, 160°C (325°F), Gas Mark 3, for about 45–50 minutes until set and lightly browned. Serve warm or cold.

Double Chocolate Tart

Serves 6–8
Preparation time 40 minutes,
  plus chilling and cooling
Cooking time 40 minutes

400 g (13 oz) chilled ready-
  made or homemade
  sweet shortcrust pastry (see
  page 9)
150 g (5 oz) plain dark
  chocolate, broken into
  pieces, plus 50 g (2 oz) to
  decorate
150 g (5 oz) white chocolate
100 g (3½ oz) unsalted butter
3 eggs
1 egg yolk
100 g (3½ oz) caster sugar
2 tablespoons double cream

Roll out the pastry on a lightly floured surface until large enough to line a buttered 24 cm (9½ inch) fluted, loose-bottomed flan tin. Lift over a rolling pin, drape into the tin and press over the base and sides. Trim off the excess pastry, prick the base with a fork, then chill for 15 minutes. Line with nonstick baking paper, add baking beans and bake in a preheated oven, 190°C (375°F), Gas Mark 5, for 15 minutes. Remove the paper and beans and bake for a further 5 minutes. Remove from the oven and reduce the oven temperature to 160°C (325°F), Gas Mark 3.

Melt the dark and white chocolate in separate bowls over a saucepan of simmering water (see page 51). Add three-quarters of the butter to the dark chocolate and the rest to the white chocolate. Leave until melted.

Whisk the eggs, egg yolk and sugar in a third bowl for 3–4 minutes until doubled in volume (but not so thick as to leave a trail). Fold two-thirds into the dark chocolate mixture, then pour into the cooked tart case. Fold the cream into the white chocolate to loosen it, then fold in the remaining whisked egg mixture. Spoon over the dark chocolate layer to completely cover.

Cook the tart for 20 minutes until just set with a slight wobble to the centre. Cool for at least 1 hour. Pipe double lines of melted dark chocolate and leave for at least 30 minutes before serving.

French Onion Tarts

Makes 12
Preparation time 30 minutes,
   plus chilling
Cooking time 30–35 minutes

1 quantity all-butter shortcrust
   pastry (see page 9)
50 g (2 oz) butter
2 onions, thinly sliced
4 eggs
200 ml (7 fl oz) milk
2 teaspoons Dijon mustard
125 g (4 oz) Gruyère cheese,
   finely grated
salt and pepper

Roll the pastry out thinly on a lightly floured surface, then stamp out 12 x 10 cm (4 inch) circles, with a plain biscuit cutter, and press into a buttered 12-section muffin tin. Reknead and reroll the pastry trimmings as needed. Chill for 15 minutes.

Heat the butter in a frying pan, add the onions and fry over a gentle heat for 10 minutes, stirring from time to time until softened and just beginning to colour.

Add the eggs, milk and mustard to a large wide-necked jug, and fork together until just mixed. Add the cheese and seasoning and mix together. Divide the mixture between the pastry cases, then spoon in the fried onions. Bake in a preheated oven, 190°C (375°F), Gas Mark 5, for 20–25 minutes until golden brown and just set. Leave to cool for 10 minutes, then loosen the edges of the tarts with a knife and remove from the tins. Serve warm or cold with salad.

Sausage Slice

Serves 6
Preparation time 25 minutes,
 plus chilling
Cooking time 30–45 minutes

1 tablespoon olive oil
1 small onion, chopped
500 g (1 lb) sausagemeat
1 teaspoon dried mixed herbs
1 egg, beaten
400 g (13 oz) chilled ready-
 made puff pastry
1 small cooking apple,
 peeled, cored and sliced
salt and pepper

Heat the oil in a small frying pan and fry the onion until soft. Tip into a bowl, cool slightly, and then add the sausagemeat and herbs. Season and stir in half the beaten egg.

Roll out three-quarters of the pastry to a 25 cm (10 inch) square and place on a greased baking sheet. Spread the sausagemeat mixture over the pastry to within 1 cm (½ inch) of the edge. Arrange the slice apple on top. Dampen the edges of the pastry with water.

Roll out the remaining pastry. Cut into 1 cm (½ inch) wide strips and make a woven trellis over the top of the apple. Brush with the remaining beaten egg and chill in the refrigerator for 30 minutes.

Bake a preheated oven, 220°C (425°F), Gas Mark 7, for 15 minutes. Reduce the temperature to 180°C (350°F), Gas Mark 4, and cook for a further 15–30 minutes until golden.

Venison & Red Wine Pie

Serves 4
Preparation time 25 minutes
Cooking time 2 hours
  50 minutes

1 tablespoon olive oil
650 g (1 lb 5 oz) shoulder or
  leg venison, diced
1 onion, chopped
4 streaky bacon rashers, diced
2 garlic cloves, finely chopped
2 tablespoons plain flour
300 ml (½ pint) red wine
450 ml (¾ pint) beef stock
1 tablespoon tomato purée
3 sprigs rosemary, leaves
  chopped, plus extra, torn,
  for sprinkling
25 g (1 oz) butter
300 g (10 oz) shallots, peeled
  and halved if large
150 g (5 oz) closed-cup
  mushrooms, thickly sliced
1 quantity rosemary shortcrust
  pastry (see page 9)
beaten egg, to glaze
salt and pepper

Heat the oil in a flameproof casserole, add the venison, then add the onion and bacon, and fry, stirring, until the venison is browned. Stir in the garlic and flour, then mix in the wine, stock and tomato purée. Add the rosemary and season well with salt and pepper.

Bring to the boil, stirring, then cover and transfer to a preheated oven, 160°C (325°F), Gas Mark 3, for 2 hours. Take the dish out of the oven. Heat the butter in a frying pan, add the shallots and mushrooms and fry until golden, then stir into the venison and leave to cool.

Spoon the venison mixture into a 1.2 litre (2 pint) ovenproof pie dish. Roll out the pastry on a lightly floured surface until about 5 cm (2 inches) wider than the diameter of the pie dish. Cut 2 long strips from the edges about 1 cm (½ inch) wide. Brush the dish rim with egg, press the strips on top, then brush these with egg. Lift the pie lid in place, sealing the edges together well. Trim off the excess pastry.

Trim off the excess pastry. Press your first and second finger on to the pie edge, then make small cuts between them with a small knife to create a scalloped edge. Repeat all the way around the pie. Brush with egg and sprinkle with a few extra torn rosemary leaves. Decorate the top if liked. Bake in a preheated oven, 190°C (375°F), Gas Mark 5, for 35–40 minutes until the pastry is golden and the filling piping hot.

Chicken & Mushroom Pies

Makes 4
Preparation time 35 minutes,
  plus chilling
Cooking time 1 hour
  10 minutes

1 tablespoon olive oil
8 boneless, skinless chicken
  thighs, about 625 g (1¼ lb),
  cubed
1 onion, chopped
2 garlic cloves, finely chopped
2 tablespoons plain flour
150 ml (¼ pint) white wine
200 ml (7 fl oz) chicken stock
few sprigs thyme or a little
  dried thyme
25 g (1 oz) butter
125 g (4 oz) closed-cup
  mushrooms, sliced
beaten egg, to glaze
salt and pepper

Heat the oil in a large frying pan and fry the chicken, stirring, until beginning to colour. Add the onion and fry until the chicken is golden and the onion softened. Stir in the garlic, then mix in the flour. Add the wine, stock, thyme and a generous sprinkle of salt and pepper. Bring to the boil, stirring, then cover and simmer for 30 minutes.

Heat the butter in a small frying pan, add the mushrooms and fry until golden. Add to the chicken and leave to cool.

To make the pastry, add the flour, mustard and a little salt and pepper to a mixing bowl. Add the fats and rub in using your fingertips or using an electric mixer until you have fine crumbs. Gradually mix in enough of the water to form a soft but not sticky dough. Knead lightly, wrap in clingfilm and chill for 15 minutes.

Reserve one-third of the pastry, then cut the rest into 4 pieces. Roll each piece out thinly, then line 4 buttered individual springform tins, 10 cm (4 inches) in diameter and 4.5 cm (1¾ inches) deep. Roll out the reserved pastry thinly and cut out lids, using the tins as a guide.

Pastry

300 g (10 oz) plain flour
1½ teaspoons dry mustard
    powder
150 g (5 oz) mixed butter and
    white vegetable fat, diced
3 tablespoons cold water
salt and pepper

Spoon the chicken filling into the pies, brush the top edges with beaten egg, then add the lids and press the pastry edges together. Flute the edges and bake on a baking sheet in a preheated oven, 190°C (375°C), Gas Mark 5, for 30 minutes until golden. Leave to stand for 5 minutes, then loosen the edges, transfer to a plate and remove the tins.

Cockle, Leek & Bacon Pies

Makes 6
Preparation time 45 minutes,
  plus chilling
Cooking time 50–55 minutes

600 ml (1 pint) milk
200 g (7 oz) leeks, trimmed,
  thinly sliced, white and
  green parts kept separate
2 bay leaves
250 g (8 oz) gammon steak
50 g (2 oz) butter
50 g (2 oz) plain flour
200 g (7 oz) cockles, defrosted
  if frozen
beaten egg, to glaze
salt and pepper

Pastry
375 g (12 oz) plain flour
175 g (6 oz) mixed butter and
  white vegetable fat, diced
4–4½ tablespoons cold water
salt and pepper

Place the milk, white sliced leeks, bay leaves, salt and pepper in a saucepan and bring to the boil. Set aside for 10 minutes. Grill the gammon on a foil-lined grill pan for 7–8 minutes, turning once. Trim off the fat, then dice the meat.

Heat the butter in a saucepan, stir in the flour, cook for 1–2 minutes, then gradually mix in the strained milk. Bring to the boil, stirring until smooth. Discard the bay leaves, then return the white leeks to the sauce, add the green sliced leeks and cook gently for 2–3 minutes, stirring until the leeks are just cooked. Leave to cool.

Make the pastry according to the method on page 9. Wrap in clingfilm and chill for 15 minutes. Reserve one-third of the pastry, roll out the remainder thinly. Cut 6 × 15 cm (6 inch) circles and press into buttered individual tart tins, 10 cm (4 inches) in diameter and 2.5 cm (1 inch) deep. Trim off excess pastry and reroll the trimmings as needed.

Stir the cockles and gammon into the sauce and spoon into the pastry bases. Brush the edges with egg. Roll out the reserved pastry and cut 12 cm (5 inch) circles for the lids. Trim off the excess pastry. Press your first and second finger on to the pic edge, then make small cuts between them with a small knife to create a scalloped edge. Repeat all the way around the pie. Prick the top and brush with beaten egg. Decorate the top if liked and sprinkle with salt and pepper. Bake the pies on a baking sheet in a preheated oven, 190°C (375°F), Gas Mark 5, for 30–35 minutes until golden brown.

Scones & Muffins

Orange & Sultana Scones
Wholewheat Treacle Scones
Griddle Cakes
Drop Scones
Vanilla Chocolate Chip Muffins
Chocolate Muffins
Wholemeal Banana & Walnut Muffins
Fruity Lunchbox Muffins
Blueberry Muffins
Almond & Pear Muffins
Overnight Muffins
Spicy Cheese & Parsnip Muffins
Tomato & Olive Muffins
Yogurt, Cheddar & Rosemary Muffins

Orange & Sultana Scones

Makes 10
Preparation time 20 minutes
Cooking time 10 minutes

375 g (12 oz) self-raising flour
50 g (2 oz) butter, diced
50 g (2 oz) caster sugar, plus
    extra for sprinkling
75 g (3 oz) sultanas
grated rind of 1 orange
1 egg, beaten
150–200 ml (5–7 fl oz)
    semi-skimmed milk

To serve
5 tablespoons apricot jam
2 x 113 g (3¾ oz) packets
    clotted cream

Put the flour in a mixing bowl or a food processor. Add the butter and rub in with your fingertips or process until the mixture resembles fine breadcrumbs. Stir in the sugar, sultanas and orange rind. Add all but 1 tablespoon of the egg then gradually mix in enough of the milk to mix to a soft but not sticky dough.

Knead lightly then roll out on a lightly floured surface until 1.5 cm (¾ inch) thick. Stamp out 5.5 cm (2¼ inch) circles using a plain round biscuit cutter. (Don't be tempted to roll out the dough thinner and make more scones as they will just look mean and miserly.) Transfer to a lightly greased baking sheet. Reknead the trimmings and continue rolling and stamping out until you have made 10 scones.

Brush the tops with the reserved egg and sprinkle lightly with a little extra caster sugar. Bake in a preheated oven, 200°C (400°F), Gas Mark 6, for 10–12 minutes until well risen and golden. Leave to cool on the baking sheet. Serve warm or just cold, split and filled with jam and clotted cream. They are best eaten on the day they are made.

Wholewheat Treacle Scones

Makes 14
Preparation time 15 minutes
Cooking time 6–8 minutes

400 g (13 oz) malted bread
  flour, plus extra for
  sprinkling (optional)
50 g (2 oz) butter, diced
50 g (2 oz) light muscovado
  sugar
3 teaspoons baking powder
1 teaspoon bicarbonate of
  soda
8 tablespoons low-fat natural
  yogurt
2 tablespoons black treacle
1 egg, beaten

To serve
500 ml (17 fl oz) carton crème
  fraîche
375 g (13 fl oz) jar strawberry
  jam

Put the flour in a mixing bowl or a food processor. Add the butter and rub in with your fingertips or process until the mixture resembles fine breadcrumbs. Stir in the sugar and baking powder.

Stir the bicarbonate of soda into the yogurt then add to the flour mixture with the black treacle. Gradually mix in enough of the beaten egg to form a soft but not sticky dough. Knead lightly then roll out on a lightly floured surface until 2 cm (¾ inch) thick.

Working quickly, cut out 5.5 cm (2¼ inch) circles using a plain biscuit cutter. Transfer to a greased baking sheet. Reknead the trimmings and continue rolling and stamping out until all the mixture has been used. Add to the baking sheet and sprinkle the tops with a little extra flour or leave plain if preferred.

Bake in a preheated oven, 220°C (425°F), Gas Mark 7, for 6–8 minutes until well risen and browned. Serve warm or cold, split and topped with crème fraîche and jam. They are best eaten on the day they are made.

Griddle Cakes

Makes 30
Preparation time 25 minutes
Cooking time 18 minutes

250 g (8 oz) self-raising flour
125 g (4 oz) butter, diced
100 g (3½ oz) caster sugar,
   plus extra for sprinkling
50 g (2 oz) currants
50 g (2 oz) sultanas
1 teaspoon ground mixed
   spice
grated rind of ½ lemon
1 egg, beaten
1 tablespoon milk, if needed
oil, for greasing

Put the flour in a mixing bowl or a food processor. Add
the butter and rub in with your fingertips or process until
the mixture resembles fine breadcrumbs. Stir in the sugar,
dried fruit, spice and lemon rind.

Add the egg then gradually mix in milk, if needed, to make
a smooth dough. Knead lightly then roll out on a lightly
floured surface until 5 mm (¼ inch) thick. Stamp out 5 cm
(2 inch) circles using a fluted round biscuit cutter. Reknead
the trimmings and continue rolling and stamping out until
all the dough has been used.

Pour a little oil on to a piece of folded kitchen paper and use to grease a griddle or heavy nonstick frying pan. Heat the pan then add the cakes in batches, regreasing the griddle or pan as needed, and fry over a medium to low heat for about 3 minutes each side until golden brown and cooked through. Serve warm, sprinkled with a little extra sugar or spread with butter, if liked. Store in an airtight tin for up to 2 days.

Drop Scones

Makes 18
Preparation time 10 minutes
Cooking time 6–7 minutes
    per batch

125 g (4 oz) self-raising flour
2 tablespoons caster sugar
1 egg, beaten
about 150 ml (¼ pint) milk

Sift the flour into a mixing bowl and mix in the sugar. Make a well in the centre and pour in the egg. Stir in the milk gradually and mix to creamy batter. The thicker the batter, the thicker the drop scones will be.

Heat a griddle and grease it lightly. Using a large spoon, drop the batter off the point in round 'puddles' on to the griddle, leaving space for spreading. Cook over a moderate heat until the top surface is covered with bubbles. When the underneath is golden, turn over with a palette knife and cook the other side. When golden, lift off the griddle and wrap in a clean tea towel or napkin.

Serve as soon as possible with butter, honey and preserves. Any drop scones that are left over can be crisped under a medium grill before serving the next day.

Vanilla Chocolate Chip Muffins

Makes 12
Preparation time 10 minutes
Cooking time 18–20 minutes

300 g (10 oz) self-raising flour
1 teaspoon baking powder
50 g (2 oz) cold unsalted
   butter, cut into small pieces
80 g (3 oz) caster sugar
150 g (5 oz) milk or plain
   chocolate chips
2 eggs, lightly beaten
225 ml (7½ fl oz) milk
1 teaspoon vanilla extract

Mix the flour and baking powder together in a large bowl. Rub in the butter until the mixture resembles fine breadcrumbs. Stir in the sugar and chocolate chips.

In a separate bowl or jug, mix the eggs, milk and vanilla extract together, then pour the egg mixture all at once into the dry ingredients and mix briefly until just combined. Line a 12-section muffin tray with paper cases. Spoon the batter into the muffin cases, dividing it evenly.

Bake in a preheated oven, 200°C (400°F), Gas Mark 6, for 18–20 minutes, or until well risen, golden and firm to the touch. Cool in the tin for 10 minutes, then turn out onto a wire rack. Serve warm or cold.

Chocolate Muffins

Makes 12
Preparation time 15 minutes
Cooking time 25 minutes

375 g (12 oz) self-raising flour
25 g (1 oz) cocoa powder
200 g (7 oz) golden caster
  sugar
2 large eggs
150 ml (¼ pint) sunflower oil
150 ml (¼ pint) milk
1 teaspoon vanilla extract
12 teaspoons chocolate
  hazelnut spread

Sieve the flour and cocoa powder into a bowl and add the sugar, stirring to mix. Combine the eggs, sunflower oil, milk and vanilla extract in a jug, using a fork. Pour the wet ingredients into the dry and stir a few times until the ingredients are just combined.

Line a 12-section muffin tray with paper cases. Half-fill the muffin cases with muffin mixture, add 1 teaspoon chocolate spread to each case and then top with the rest of the muffin mixture.

Bake in a preheated oven, 190°C (375°F), Gas Mark 5, for 25 minutes until the muffins are well risen and springy to the touch.

Wholemeal Banana & Walnut Muffins

Makes 12
Preparation time 10 minutes
Cooking time 20 minutes

150 g (5 oz) self-raising
  wholemeal flour
150 g (5 oz) self-raising
  white flour
2 tablespoons soft light
  brown sugar
65 g (2½ oz) walnuts,
  chopped
3 large very ripe bananas,
  peeled
3 tablespoons sunflower oil
2 eggs, lightly beaten
5 tablespoons soured cream
2 tablespoons clear honey

Grease a 12-section muffin tray or line with paper muffin cases. Mix both the flours, sugar and walnuts together in a large bowl.

In a separate bowl, mash the bananas until fairly smooth using a potato masher or fork, then stir in the sunflower oil, eggs, soured cream and honey.

Add the wet ingredients all at once to the dry ingredients and mix briefly until just combined. Spoon the batter into the muffin cases, dividing it evenly.

Bake in a preheated oven, 200°C (400°F), Gas Mark 6, for about 20 minutes, or until risen and golden. Cool in the tin for 10 minutes, then turn out onto a wire rack. Serve warm or cold.

Fruity Lunchbox Muffins

Makes 12
Preparation time 10 minutes
Cooking time 15 minutes

100 g (3½ oz) plain flour
100 g (3½ oz) wholemeal flour
2 teaspoons baking powder
75 g (3 oz) golden caster sugar
2 eggs
2 tablespoons mild olive oil or vegetable oil
40 g (1½ oz) lightly salted butter, melted
2 teaspoons vanilla extract
150 g (5 oz) red fruit yogurt, such as strawberry, raspberry or cherry
100 g (½ oz) fresh raspberries or strawberries, cut into small pieces

Line a 12-section muffin tray with paper muffin cases. Put both the flours, baking powder and sugar in a bowl.

Whisk together the eggs, oil, melted butter, vanilla extract and yogurt with a fork in a jug and add to the bowl. Mix gently with a large metal spoon until the ingredients have started to blend together. Scatter with half the berry pieces and mix a little more until the ingredients are only just combined. Divide the muffin mixture between the muffin cases. Scatter with the remaining berry pieces.

Bake in a preheated oven, 200°C (400°F), Gas Mark 6, for 15 minutes or until well risen and just firm. Transfer to a wire rack to cool.

Blueberry Muffins

Makes 12
Preparation time 10 minutes
Cooking time 20 minutes

300 g (10 oz) self-raising flour
1 teaspoon baking powder
50 g (2 oz) cold unsalted
    butter, cut into pieces
80 g (3 oz) caster sugar
150 g fresh blueberries
2 eggs, lightly beaten
225 ml (7½ fl oz) milk
1 teaspoon vanilla extract

Grease a 12-section muffin tray or line with paper muffin cases. Mix the flour and baking powder together in a large bowl. Rub in the butter until the mixture resembles fine breadcrumbs. Stir the sugar and blueberries into this mixture.

In a separate small bowl or jug, mix the eggs, milk and vanilla extract together. Pour the egg mixture all at once into the dry ingredients and mix briefly until just combined.

Spoon the batter into the muffin cases, dividing it evenly. Bake in a preheated oven, 200°C (400°F), Gas Mark 6, for about 20 minutes, or until risen and golden. Cool in the tin for 10 minutes, then turn out onto a wire rack. Serve warm or cold.

Almond & Pear Muffins

Makes 12
Preparation time 10 minutes
Cooking time 18–20 minutes

300 g (10 oz) plain flour
1 tablespoon baking powder
¼ teaspoon freshly grated
    nutmeg
4 tablespoons ground
    almonds
100 g (3½ oz) blanched
    almonds, chopped
100 g (3½ oz) marzipan, cut
    into small pieces
150 g (5 oz) soft light brown
    sugar
1 egg, lightly beaten
200 ml (7 fl oz) unsweetened
    pear or apple juice
75 g (3 oz) unsalted butter,
    melted
2 small ripe pears, peeled,
    cored and chopped
25 g (1 oz) flaked almonds
sifted icing sugar, for dusting

Grease a 12-section muffin tray or line twith paper muffin cases. Mix the flour, baking powder, nutmeg, ground and chopped almonds, marzipan and brown sugar together in a large bowl.

In a separate bowl or jug, mix the egg, pear or apple juice, melted butter and pears together. Add the pear mixture all at once to the dry ingredients and mix briefly until just combined.

Spoon the batter into the prepared muffin cases, dividing it evenly, then sprinkle the tops with the flaked almonds. Bake in a preheated oven, 190°C (375°F), Gas Mark 5, for 18–20 minutes, or until well risen and golden.

Cool in the tin for 5 minutes, then turn out onto a wire rack. Dust with sifted icing sugar and serve warm or cold.

Overnight Muffins

Makes 12
Preparation time 10 minutes
Cooking time 20 minutes

225 g (7½ oz) plain flour
25 g (1 oz) oat bran
100 g (3½ oz) unsweetened
   muesli
100 g (3½ oz) soft brown sugar
1½ teaspoons ground
   cinnamon
1 teaspoon bicarbonate
   of soda
100 g (3½ oz) ready-to-eat
   dried apricots or dried
   dates, chopped
1 egg lightly beaten
375 ml (13 fl oz) buttermilk
125 ml (4 fl oz) vegetable oil
2 tablespoons demerara sugar

Mix the flour, oat bran, muesli, brown sugar, cinnamon, bicarbonate of soda and dried apricots or dates in a large bowl. In a separate bowl of jug, mix together the egg, buttermilk and vegetable oil.

Pour the wet ingredients into the dry ingredients and mix briefly until just combined. Cover the bowl with clingfilm and refrigerate for at least 8 hours or overnight.

When ready to bake, grease a 12-section muffin tray or line with paper muffin cases. Divide the mixture between the cases and sprinkle the demerara sugar evenly over the tops. Bake in a preheated oven, 190°C (375°F), Gas Mark 5, for 20 minutes or until risen and golden. Cool in the tray for 10 minutes, then turn out onto a wire rack. Serve warm or cold.

Spicy Cheese & Parsnip Muffins

Makes 10
Preparation time 20 minutes,
  plus cooling
Cooking time 30 minutes

250 g (8 oz) parsnips, diced
approximately 225 ml (7 fl oz)
  milk
4 tablespoons olive oil
1 egg, beaten
1 teaspoon Tabasco sauce
2 teaspoons pink
  peppercorns, crushed
275 g (9 oz) plain flour
1 tablespoon baking powder
75 g (3 oz) Gruyère cheese,
  finely grated
salt

Line 10 sections of a 12-section muffin tray with paper muffin cases. Cook the parsnips in a saucepan of lightly salted boiling water for 10 minutes until tender. Drain, mash and leave to cool.

Beat the milk into the cooled parsnips along with the oil, egg, Tabasco sauce and 1 teaspoon of the peppercorns, adding a dash more milk if the mixture feels dry.

Put the flour, baking powder, ½ teaspoon salt and all but 1 tablespoon of the cheese in a large bowl and mix well. Add the parsnip mixture and stir with a large metal spoon until the ingredients are only just combined.

Divide the muffin mixture between the muffin cases and sprinkle with the remaining cheese, peppercorns and a little extra salt. Bake in a preheated oven, 220°C (425°F), Gas Mark 7, for 20 minutes or until risen and pale golden. Transfer to a wire rack. Serve warm or cold.

Tomato & Olive Muffins

Makes 12
Preparation time 10 minutes
Cooking time 20 minutes

300 g (10 oz) plain flour
1 tablespoon baking powder
1 tablespoon caster sugar
25 g (1 oz) fresh Parmesan
   cheese, finely grated
3 tablespoons chopped basil
1 egg, lightly beaten
175 ml (6 fl oz) milk
100 g (3½ oz) unsalted butter,
   melted
1 tablespoon olive oil
4 medium tomatoes, skinned,
   seeded and chopped
50 g (2 oz) pitted mixed black
   and green olives, roughly
   chopped
1 clove garlic, crushed
salt and freshly ground black
   pepper, to taste

Topping
40 g (1½ oz) fresh white
   breadcrumbs
25 g (1 oz) fresh Parmesan
   cheese, finely grated
2 teaspoons poppy seeds

Line a 12-section muffin tray with paper muffin cases. Mix the flour, baking powder, sugar, Parmesan and basil together in a large bowl. In a separate bowl, mix the egg, milk, melted butter, olive oil, tomatoes, olives, garlic and salt and pepper together. Pour the tomato mixture all at once into the dry ingredients and mix briefly until just combined.

Spoon the batter into the muffin cases, dividing it evenly. For the topping, mix all the ingredients together in a bowl. Sprinkle this mixture over the tops of the muffins.

Bake in a preheated oven, 200°C (400°F), Gas Mark 6, for about 20 minutes or until well risen and lightly browned. Cool in the tin for 5 minutes, then turn out onto a wire rack. Serve warm or cold.

Yogurt, Cheddar & Rosemary Muffins

Makes 12
Preparation time 20 minutes
Cooking time 20–25 minutes

250 g (8 oz) wholemeal bread flour

125 g (4 oz) white bread flour

125 g (4 oz) buckwheat flour

2 teaspoons salt

1½ teaspoons baking powder

½ teaspoon bicarbonate of soda

2 tablespoons chopped fresh rosemary

50 g (2 oz) melted butter

2 eggs, beaten

100 ml (3½ fl oz) natural yogurt

100 ml (3½ fl oz) milk

75 g (3 oz) Cheddar cheese, grated

8 small sprigs fresh rosemary

Mix all the dry ingredients together in the bowl of a food mixer and make a well in the centre. Beat together the remaining ingredients (except the rosemary sprigs) and pour them into the dry ingredients. Set the mixer to low and work the ingredients until they form a sticky dough.

Lightly oil an 8-section mini-loaf tin or muffin tray. Take large spoonfuls of the mixture and press into the prepared tins. Press a rosemary sprig into each one.

Bake in a preheated oven, 190°C (375°F), Gas Mark 5, for 20–25 minutes until risen and lightly golden. Leave to cool in the tins for 5 minutes, then transfer to a wire rack to cool.

Bread & Rolls

Cottage Loaf
Farmhouse White Loaf
Quick White Loaf
Granary Bread
Quick Wholemeal Loaf
Mixed Seed Bread
Bacon & Beer Soda Bread
Fig & Walnut Bread
Wholemeal Rolls
Fancy Rolls
Orange & Poppy Seed Buns
Tea Cakes

Cottage Loaf

Makes 1 large loaf
Preparation time 30 minutes,
   plus proving
Cooking time 30 minutes

750 g (1½ lb) white bread
   flour, sifted
7 g (¼ oz) sachet fast-acting
   dried yeast
2 teaspoons salt
1 teaspoon caster sugar
15 g (½ oz) chilled butter,
   diced
50 ml (¾ pint) warm water
extra flour, for kneading and
   shaping

Combine the flour, yeast, salt and sugar in the bowl of a food mixer. Rub in the butter. Add the water and with the mixer set to low work the ingredients until they just come together. Increase speed to high and knead dough for 8–10 minutes until smooth and elastic. (If making dough by hand, bring ingredients together in a bowl to form a soft dough. Knead on a lightly floured surface for 8–10 minutes. Continue as above.)

Shape dough into a ball and put in an oiled bowl, cover with a tea towel and leave to rise in a warm place for 1 hour until doubled in size.

On a lightly floured surface, knock back the dough, shape into an oval and press, seam side down in an oiled 1 kg (2 lb) loaf tin. Cover with oiled clingfilm and leave to rise for 30 minutes more until dough reaches the top of the tin.

Bake in a preheated oven, 230°C (450°F), Gas Mark 8, for 15 minutes. Reduce oven to 200°C (400°F), Gas Mark 6, and bake for 15 minutes more until risen and hollow sounding when tapped underneath. Cool on a rack.

Farmhouse White Loaf

Makes 1 large loaf
Preparation time 30 minutes,
  plus proving
Cooking time 30 minutes

475 g (15 oz) strong white
  flour
2 tablespoons butter
1½ teaspoons sugar
1 teaspoon salt
1¼ teaspoons fast-acting
  dried yeast
275 ml (9 fl oz) warm water

Put the flour into a large bowl, add the butter and rub in with the fingertips until the mixture resembles fine breadcrumbs. Stir in the sugar, salt and yeast. Gradually mix in enough warm water to make a soft dough.

Knead well on a lightly floured surface for 5 minutes until the dough is smooth and elastic. Put the dough back into the bowl, cover loosely with oiled clingfilm and leave in a warm place to rise for 45 minutes or until doubled in size.

Tip the dough out on to a lightly floured surface, knead well then put into a greased 1 kg (2 lb) loaf tin. Cover loosely with oiled clingfilm and leave in a warm place to rise for 30 minutes or until the dough reaches the top of the tin.

Remove the clingfilm, sprinkle with flour and bake in a preheated oven, 200°C (400°F), Gas Mark 6, for 30 minutes, covering with foil after 20 minutes to prevent overbrowning.

Holding the tin with oven gloves, loosen the bread with a palette knife. Transfer to a wire rack to cool.

Quick White Loaf

Makes 1 large loaf
Preparation time 30 minutes, plus proving
Cooking time 30 minutes

500 g (1 lb) strong white flour
2 tablespoons milk powder
1 tablespoon caster sugar
1 teaspoon salt
2½ teaspoons fast-acting dried yeast
2 tablespoons sunflower oil
300 ml (½ pint) warm water

Mix the flour, milk powder, sugar, salt and yeast in a large bowl. Add the oil and gradually mix in enough warm water to make a soft dough.

Knead well on a lightly floured surface for 10 minutes until the dough is smooth and elastic. Put into a greased 1 kg (2 lb) loaf tin. Cover loosely with oiled clingfilm and leave in a warm place to rise for 45 minutes or until the dough reaches just above the top of the tin.

Remove the clingfilm and bake in a preheated oven, 200°C (400°F), Gas Mark 6, for 30 minutes, or until the bread is golden brown and sounds hollow when tapped with the fingertips. Check loaf after 15 minutes and cover with foil if overbrowning.

Holding the tin with oven gloves, loosen the bread with a palette knife. Transfer to a wire rack to cool.

Granary Bread

Makes 1 large loaf
Preparation time 30 minutes,
    plus proving
Cooking time 30–35 minutes

500 g (1 lb) granary flour
2 tablespoons butter
1½ teaspoons salt
1 tablespoon brown sugar
1¼ teaspoons fast-acting
    dried yeast
300 ml (½ pint) water

Put the flour into a large bowl, add the butter and rub in with the fingertips until the mixture resembles fine breadcrumbs. Stir in the salt, sugar and yeast then gradually mix in enough warm water to make a soft dough.

Knead on a lightly floured surface for 5 minutes until the dough is smooth and elastic. Put back into the bowl, cover loosely with oiled clingfilm and leave in a warm place to rise for 1 hour or until doubled in size.

Tip the dough out on to a lightly floured surface and knead well, adding flour to the surface to stop the dough sticking, if needed. Press into a greased 1 kg (2 lb) loaf tin. Cover loosely with oiled clingfilm and leave in a warm place to rise for 30 minutes or until the dough reaches the top of the tin.

Remove the clingfilm and bake in a preheated oven, 200°C (400°F), Gas Mark 6, for 30–35 minutes, or until the bread is browned and sounds hollow when tapped with the fingertips. Check after 15 minutes and cover with foil if overbrowning.

Holding the tin with oven gloves, loosen the bread with a palette knife. Transfer to a wire rack to cool.

Quick Wholemeal Loaf

Makes 1 large loaf
Preparation time 30 minutes,
  plus proving
Cooking time 30 minutes

250 g (8 oz) strong wholemeal
  flour
250 g (8 oz) strong white flour
1 tablespoon caster sugar
1 teaspoon salt
2½ teaspoons fast-acting
  dried yeast
2 tablespoons sunflower oil
300 ml (½ pint) warm water

Mix the flours, sugar, salt and yeast in a large bowl. Add the oil and gradually mix in enough warm water to make a soft dough.

Knead well on a lightly floured surface for 10 minutes until the dough is smooth and elastic. Put into a greased 1 kg (2 lb) loaf tin. Cover loosely with oiled clingfilm and leave in a warm place to rise for 45 minutes or until the dough reaches just above the top of the tin.

Remove the clingfilm and bake in a preheated oven, 200°C (400°F), Gas Mark 6, for 30 minutes, or until the bread is browned and sounds hollow when tapped with the fingertips. Check after 15 minutes and cover with foil if the top is overbrowning.

Holding the tin with oven gloves, loosen the bread with a palette knife. Transfer to a wire rack to cool.

Mixed Seed Bread

Makes 1 large loaf
Preparation time 30 minutes,
  plus proving
Cooking time 30–35 minutes

475 g (15 oz) malthouse flour
2 tablespoons butter
1 tablespoon brown sugar
1½ teaspoons salt
3 tablespoons sesame seeds
3 tablespoons sunflower
  seeds
3 tablespoons linseeds
1¼ teaspoons fast-acting
  dried yeast
300 ml (½ pint) water
milk to glaze
extra seeds, optional

Put the flour into a large bowl, add the butter and rub in with the fingertips until the mixture resembles fine breadcrumbs. Stir in the sugar, salt, seeds and yeast. Gradually mix in enough warm water to make a soft dough.

Knead well on a lightly floured surface for 5 minutes until the dough is smooth and elastic. Put back into the bowl, cover loosely with oiled clingfilm and leave in a warm place to rise for 1 hour or until doubled in size.

Turn out on to a lightly floured surface and knead again for 5 minutes. Put the dough into a greased 20 cm (8 inch) round loose-bottomed tin. Cover loosely with oiled clingfilm and leave in a warm place to rise for 30 minutes or until the dough reaches the top of the tin.

Remove the clingfilm, brush the top with a little milk and sprinkle with some extra seeds. Bake in a preheated oven, 200°C (400°F), Gas Mark 6, for 30–35 minutes or until the bread is well risen, golden and sounds hollow when tapped. Cover with foil after 15 minutes to prevent overbrowning.

Holding the tin with oven gloves, loosen the bread with a palette knife. Transfer to a wire rack to cool.

Bacon & Beer Soda Bread

Makes 1 small loaf
Preparation time 30 minutes
Cooking time 35–40 minutes

125 g (4 oz) smoked bacon,
  finely chopped,
350 g (12 oz) wholemeal
  bread flour
125 g (4 oz) medium oatmeal
2 teaspoons baking powder
1½ teaspoons bicarbonate
  of soda
1 teaspoon salt
300 ml (½ pint) light beer
2 tablespoons vegetable oil

Dry-fry the bacon for 3–4 minutes until golden. Set aside to cool. Combine the dry ingredients in a bowl, add the beer, oil and cooled bacon and work the ingredients together to form a soft dough. Transfer to a lightly floured surface and knead the dough for 2–3 minutes until it is smooth.

Shape the dough into a flat round, about 18 cm (7 inches) across, and transfer it to a lightly floured baking sheet. Use a sharp knife to score into 8 wedges, cutting down about 1 cm (½ inch) into the dough.

Bake in a preheated oven, 220°C (425°F), Gas Mark 7, for 15 minutes. Reduce the temperature to 190°C (375°F), Gas Mark 5, and bake for a further 20–25 minutes until the bread sounds hollow when tapped lightly underneath. Transfer to a wire rack and leave until cold.

Fig & Walnut Bread

Makes 2 round loaves
Preparation time 30 minutes,
  plus proving
Cooking time 30–35 minutes

450 g (14½ oz) white bread
  flour, sifted
250 g (8 oz) wholemeal bread
  flour
7 g (¼ oz) sachet fast-acting
  dried yeast
2 teaspoons salt
400 ml (14 fl oz) warm water
1 tablespoon molasses
125 g (4 oz) walnuts, toasted
  and chopped
125 g (4 oz) dried figs, finely
  chopped

Put the flours in the bowl of a food mixer and stir in the yeast and salt. Add the water and molasses, set the mixer to low and work the ingredients together to form a slightly sticky dough. Increase the speed to high and knead for 8–10 minutes until the dough is smooth and elastic. Add the walnuts and figs and knead for a further 2 minutes until evenly incorporated. (If you are making the bread by hand bring the flours, yeast, salt, warm water and molasses together in a bowl to form a soft dough. Knead on a lightly floured surface for 8–10 minutes working the walnuts and figs in towards the end.)

Shape the dough into a ball and put it in an oiled bowl. Cover with a clean tea towel and leave to rise in a warm place for 1–1½ hours or until it has doubled in size.

Turn out the dough and knock out the air. Divide the dough in 2 and form each half into a small, slightly flattened round.

Put the rounds on a large, floured baking sheet, cover loosely with oiled clingfilm and leave to rise for a further 30–45 minutes until they have doubled in size.

Use a sharp knife to cut a diamond pattern into each round and bake in a preheated oven, 220°C (425°F), Gas Mark 7, for 30–35 minutes until the bread has risen and sounds hollow when tapped underneath. Leave to cool on a wire rack.

Wholemeal Rolls

Makes 8 large rolls
Preparation time 30 minutes,
 plus proving
Cooking time 20 minutes

500 g (1 lb) wholemeal bread
 flour
250 g (8 oz) white bread flour,
 sifted
7 g (¼ oz) sachet fast-acting
 dried yeast
2 teaspoons salt
1 teaspoon caster sugar
450 ml (¾ pint) warm water
2 tablespoons milk

Put the flours, yeast, salt and sugar into the bowl of a food mixer. Add the water and, with the mixer set on low, work the ingredients until they come together to form a soft dough. Increase the speed to high and knead the dough for 8–10 minutes until it is smooth and elastic. (If you are making the rolls by hand bring the ingredients except the milk together in a large bowl to form a soft dough. Shape it into a ball and transfer to a lightly floured surface. Knead by hand for 8–10 minutes until the dough is smooth and elastic. Continue as above.)

Shape the dough into a ball and put it in an oiled bowl. Cover the bowl with a clean tea towel and leave to rise for 1 hour or until it has doubled in size.

Turn out the dough on to a lightly floured surface and knock out the air. Divide the dough into 8 equal pieces and shape these into rolls. Arrange them well spaced apart on 2 large, lightly oiled baking sheets, cover with oiled clingfilm and leave to rise for 30 minutes until they have doubled in size.

Brush the rolls with the milk and bake in a preheated oven, 220°C (425°F), Gas Mark 7, for 20 minutes until they are risen and sound hollow when tapped underneath. Leave the rolls to cool on a wire rack.

Fancy Rolls

Makes 12
Preparation time 45 minutes,
** plus proving**
Cooking time 10 minutes

475 g (15 oz) strong white
  flour
2 tablespoons butter
1 teaspoon sugar
1 teaspoon salt
1¼ teaspoons fast-acting
  dried yeast
275 ml (9 fl oz) water

To finish
1 egg yolk, to glaze
poppy or black mustard
  seeds, sesame seeds,
  fennel seeds, paprika,
  sprigs of fresh rosemary,
  coarsely ground Cajun
  spice, coarse sea salt

Put the flour into a bowl, add the butter and rub in with the fingertips until the mixture resembles fine breadcrumbs. Stir in the sugar, salt and yeast then gradually mix in enough warm water to make a soft dough.

Knead well on a lightly floured surface for 5 minutes until the dough is smooth and elastic. Put the dough back into the bowl, cover loosely with oiled clingfilm and leave in a warm place to rise for 1 hour or until doubled in size.

Tip the dough out on to a lightly floured surface, knead well then cut into 12 pieces. Shape them as opposite then put on to greased baking sheets.

Cover loosely with oiled clingfilm and leave in a warm place to rise for 20 minutes.

Remove the clingfilm, brush with the egg yolk mixed with 1 tablespoon of water and sprinkle with seeds, spices, herbs or salt. Bake in a preheated oven, 200°C (400°F), Gas Mark 6, for 10 minutes until golden and the bases sound hollow when tapped with the fingertips. Transfer to a wire rack to cool.

Coils Take 2 pieces of dough and shape each one into a rope 25 cm (10 inches) long, roll up each rope along its length to make a spiral-like coil.

Clover leaf Take 2 pieces of dough and divide each one into 3 small balls, arrange in a triangle with the balls all touching each other.

Starburst Take 2 pieces of dough and shape each into a round. Make 5 or 6 cuts with scissors towards the centre of each one to resemble the spokes of a wheel.

Knots Take 2 pieces of dough and shape each one into a rope 22 cm (9 inches) long. Loop 1 end of 1 rope then thread the other end through the loop to make the knot. Repeat.

Herb split Take 2 pieces of dough and shape into an oval. Make 4 small cuts across the top of each with scissors and insert sprigs of rosemary into them. (Add fresh sprigs after baking too.)

Orange & Poppy Seed Buns

Makes 20
Preparation time 30 minutes,
  plus proving
Cooking time 12–15 minutes

500 g (1 lb) strong white flour
2 tablespoons butter
2 tablespoons milk powder
1 teaspoon salt
3 tablespoons poppy seeds
1 orange, grated rind and
  juice
1¼ teaspoons fast-acting
  dried yeast
4 tablespoons honey
275 ml (9 fl oz) water
1 egg yolk
200 g (7 oz) icing sugar

Put the flour into a large bowl, add the butter and rub
in with the fingertips until the mixture resembles fine
breadcrumbs. Stir in the milk powder, salt, poppy seeds,
grated orange rind and yeast. Add the honey then gradually
mix in enough warm water to make a soft dough.

Knead well on a lightly floured surface for 5 minutes until
the dough is smooth and elastic. Put the dough back into
the bowl, cover loosely with oiled clingfilm and leave in a
warm place to rise for 1 hour or until doubled in size.

Tip the dough out on to a lightly floured surface, knead
well then cut into 20 pieces. Shape each piece into a small
ball and arrange, spaced well apart, on a greased baking
sheet. Cover loosely with oiled clingfilm and leave to rise
for 30 minutes or until half as big again.

Remove the clingfilm, brush with the egg yolk mixed with
1 tablespoon of water and bake in a preheated oven, 200°C
(400°F), Gas Mark 6, for 12–15 minutes until the buns are

golden and sound hollow when tapped with the fingertips. Transfer to a wire rack and leave to cool for 15 minutes.

Sift the icing sugar into a bowl then gradually mix in the juice of half the orange or enough to make a smooth spoonable icing. Drizzle the icing over the buns with a spoon making random zigzag lines. Leave for at least 15 minutes so that the icing can harden.

Tea Cakes

Makes 8
Preparation time 25 minutes, plus proving
Cooking time 20–22 minutes

500 g (1 lb) plain flour
1 teaspoon salt
2 teaspoon granulated sugar
100 g (4 oz) currants
25 g (1 oz) fresh yeast
300 ml (½ pint) warm milk
melted butter, for brushing

Sift the flour and salt in a mixing bowl and add the sugar and currants. Cream the yeast with a little extra sugar and some of the warm milk. Pour the yeast mixture into a well in the centre of the flour mixture and leave in warm place for 10 minutes. Add the remaining milk, mix to a light dough and knead well. Cover the bowl loosely with oiled clingfilm and leave in a warm place to rise for about 1–1½ hours until doubled in size.

Knead the dough again, then divide into 8 pieces and roll and shape them into tea cakes. Prick each one with a fork. Put the tea cakes on a greased baking sheet, cover with a cloth and stand in a warm place to prove for 30 minutes.

Transfer the teacakes to a preheated oven, 220°C (425°F), Gas Mark 7, and bake for 10–12 minutes. Remove from the oven, brush with melted butter, then return the tea cakes to the oven for a further 10 minutes. To serve, split each tea cake in half, toast lightly and spread with butter.

Festive Bakes

Rich Christmas Cake
Tropical Christmas Cake
Chocolate Christmas Cake
Mince Pies
Christmas Muffins
Simnel Cake
Hot Cross Buns
Easter Nests
Birthday Cake

Rich Christmas Cake

Serves 16
Preparation time 45 minutes,
   plus cooling
Cooking time 3–3½ hours

125 g (4 oz) self-raising flour
200 g (7 oz) plain flour
¼ teaspoon salt
1 teaspoon ground mixed spice
½ teaspoon ground cinnamon
½ teaspoon ground nutmeg
250 g (8 oz) butter
250 g (8 oz) soft dark brown
   or dark muscovado sugar
2 teaspoons black treacle
5 eggs
50 ml (2 fl oz) medium-dry
   sherry or strained cold tea
1½ teaspoons vanilla extract
250 g (8 oz) each currants,
   sultanas, seedless raisins
   and prunes or dates,
   roughly chopped
75 g (3 oz) cut mixed peel
50 g (2 oz) ground almonds
75 g (3 oz) glacé cherries,
   halved
finely grated rind of 1 lemon
3–4 tablespoons brandy

Grease and line a 23 cm (9 inch) round or 20 cm (8 inch) square cake tin, using a double thickness of greased greaseproof paper. Line the outside with several thicknesses of brown paper, standing at least 5 cm (2 inches) above the top of the tin.

Sift the flours into a bowl with the salt, mixed spice, cinnamon and nutmeg. In another large bowl, cream the butter with the sugar until light. Beat in the treacle.

Lightly beat together the eggs, sherry or tea and vanilla extract. Gradually beat half the egg mixture into the creamed mixture. Fold in one-third of the mixed flours. Continue to add the egg and flour mixtures alternately. Mix in all the remaining ingredients except the brandy. Turn into the prepared tin and smooth the top.

Bake in a preheated oven, 140°C (275°F), Gas Mark 1, for about 3–3½ hours until a skewer inserted into the centre of the cake comes out clean. Cover the cake with a double layer of greaseproof paper if it starts to brown too much during cooking.

Leave the cake to cool in the tin before turning out on to a wire rack to cool completely. Prick all over with a fine skewer and spoon brandy over the cake. Store the cake in an airtight tin and leave to mature for about 1 month before using.

Tropical Christmas Cake

Serves 10
Preparation time 30 minutes,
 plus cooling
Cooking time 1¼–1½ hours

300 g (10 oz) unsalted butter,
 softened
200 g (7 oz) caster sugar
3 large eggs, beaten
425 g (14 oz) self-raising flour
250 g (8 oz) pineapple rings in
 syrup
75 g (3 oz) glacé cherries,
 chopped
50 g (2 oz) cut mixed peel
3 tablespoons chopped
 angelica
3 tablespoons chopped walnuts
3 tablespoons desiccated
 coconut
75 g (3 oz) sultanas
2 tablespoons toasted coconut
 shavings, to decorate

Coconut icing
45 g (1½ oz) unsalted butter
250 g (8 oz) icing sugar
2 tablespoons desiccated
 coconut

Grease a 23 cm (9 inch) ring mould or 20 cm (8 inch) cake tin and line with nonstick baking paper or greased greaseproof paper. Cream the butter and sugar until soft and light, then gradually beat in the eggs. Sift the flour and fold into the creamed mixture.

Drain the canned pineapple, setting aside 1 tablespoon of the syrup for the icing and 3 tablespoons of the syrup for the cake. Chop the pineapple rings finely. Fold the dried fruit, nuts and pineapple into the cake mixture with the coconut, sultanas and the 3 tablespoons of pineapple syrup.

Put the mixture into the ring mould or cake tin. Bake in a preheated oven, 160°C (325°F), Gas Mark 3, for 1¼ hours if using a ring mould and 1½ hours if using a cake tin. Cool for at least 10 minutes in the tin, then turn out on to a wire rack and leave to cool completely.

Melt the butter for the icing in a pan, then remove from the heat. Sift in the icing sugar, then add the remaining pineapple syrup and the coconut. Stir to combine, then spread the icing over the top of the cake and a little down the sides. Sprinkle with toasted coconut shavings.

Chocolate Christmas Cake

Serves 20

Preparation time 1 hour, plus
soaking fruit and cooling

Cooking time 1¾ hours

250 g (8 oz) dried fruit
200 ml (7 fl oz) sherry
250 g (8 oz) butter, softened
225 g (7½ oz) molasses sugar
3 eggs
200 g (7 oz) self-raising
  wholemeal flour
50 g (2 oz) cocoa powder
2 tablespoons mixed spice
4 pieces stem ginger,
  chopped
100 g (3½ oz) white chocolate,
  chopped

To decorate
150 g (5 oz) butter, softened
150 g (5 oz) golden icing
  sugar
150 g (5 oz) cream cheese
1 tablespoon brandy
125 g (4 oz) dried cranberries

Sterilize a jar by washing it in hot, soapy water and drying in the lowest setting of your oven for 15 minutes. Fill with the dried fruit and sherry while still warm, then seal and leave to macerate for at least 1 hour and up to 1 week.

Cream the butter and sugar until fluffy. Gradually add the eggs, then sift in the flour, cocoa, mixed spice and ginger.

Whiz half the macerated fruit in a processor until smooth. Add to the cake mixture with the rest of the fruit and alcoholic liquid. Add the white chocolate and fold everything together.

Grease and line a 15 cm (6 inch) cake tin. Spoon the mixture into the tin and bake in a preheated oven, 180°C (350°F), Gas Mark 4, for 1½ hours. The cake is ready when a skewer pushed in the centre comes out clean. Cool in the tin. Put on to a plate or board and peel away the lining paper.

Blend the butter, sugar, cream cheese and brandy together in a food processor until smooth and spread on top of the cake. Finish by decorating with dried cranberries and tying a large ribbon around the sides.

Dampen the edges of the cases and press the lids down lightly to seal them. Brush the tops of the pies with a little milk or beaten egg and sprinkle lightly with the sugar. Bake in a preheated oven, 200°C (400°F), Gas Mark 6, for 20 minutes until golden. Leave to cool slightly in the tins, then transfer to a wire rack to cool completely.

Christmas Muffins

Makes 10
Preparation time 10 minutes
Cooking time 18–20 minutes

300 g (10 oz) self-raising flour
1 teaspoon baking powder
1 teaspoon ground mixed spice
100 g (3½ oz) soft light brown sugar
175 g (6 oz) mincemeat
100 g (3½ oz) unsalted butter, melted
175 ml (6 fl oz) buttermilk
1 tablespoon milk
2 teaspoons demerara sugar

Line 10 sections of a 12-section muffin tray with paper muffin cases. Mix the flour, baking powder, mixed spice and brown sugar in a large bowl. In a separate bowl or jug, mix together the mincemeat, egg, melted butter, buttermilk and milk. Add the wet ingredients to the dry and mix briefly until just combined.

Divide the mixture between the paper cases, then sprinkle the tops evenly with demerara sugar. Bake in a preheated oven, 200°C (400°F), Gas Mark 6, for 18–20 minutes or until risen and golden. Cool in the tray for 10 minutes, then turn out onto a wire rack. Serve warm or cold.

Simnel Cake

Serves 16–18
Preparation time 30 minutes
Cooking time 2–2½ hours

175 g (6 oz) unsalted butter,
  softened
175 g (6 oz) golden caster
  sugar
75 g (3 oz) fresh root ginger,
  grated
3 eggs
225 g (7½ oz) plain flour
2 teaspoons ground mixed
  spice
500 g (1 lb) mixed dried fruit
500 g (1 lb) white marzipan
icing sugar, for dusting
1 egg white, lightly beaten
physalis, to decorate

Grease and line the base and sides of an 18 cm (7 inch) round cake tin. Grease the paper. Cream together the butter, sugar and ginger until light and fluffy. Gradually beat in the eggs, adding a little of the flour if it starts to curdle. Stir in the flour and spice, then the dried fruit.

Spread half the mixture in an even layer in the tin. Roll out half the marzipan on a surface dusted with icing sugar to a round slightly smaller than the tin. Lay the paste over the cake mixture and cover with the remaining cake mix.

Bake in a preheated oven, 150°C (300°F), Gas Mark 2, for 2–2½ hours or until a skewer inserted into the centre comes out clean. Cool in the tin.

To decorate, brush the top with a little egg white. Roll out the remaining almond paste to an 18 cm (7 inch) round and lay over the cake. Crimp the edges and brush with beaten egg white. Cook under the grill, watching closely, for 2 minutes or until the paste is golden. Cool, then decorate with sugar-dusted physalis.

Hot Cross Buns

Makes 12
Preparation time 25 minutes
  plus proving
Cooking time 30–35 minutes

750 g (1½ lb) white bread
  flour, sifted
2 x 7 g (¼ oz) sachets fast-
  acting dried yeast
2 teaspoons ground mixed
  spice
1 teaspoon ground cinnamon,
100 g (3½ oz) raisins
75 g (3 oz) cut mixed peel
100 g (3½ oz) caster sugar
350 ml (12 fl oz) warm milk
50 g (2 oz) unsalted butter,
  melted
1 egg, lightly beaten

Piping paste
50 g (2 oz) plain flour
1 tablespoon caster sugar
3 tablespoons water

Apricot glaze
250 g (8 oz) apricot jam
2 teaspoons lemon juice
2 teaspoons water

Combine the sifted flour, yeast, spices, raisins, peel and sugar in the bowl of a food mixer. Add the milk, melted butter and egg. Set the mixer to low and work the ingredients together to form a soft dough. Increase the speed to high and knead for 8–10 minutes until the dough is smooth and elastic. Place the dough in an oiled bowl, cover with a clean tea towel and leave to rise in a warm place for 1 hour or until doubled in size.

Knock back the dough on a lightly floured surface. Divide into 12 equal-sized pieces and shape each one into a small bun. Press the buns into a lightly oiled 20 x 30 cm (8 x 12 inch) cake tin. Cover with oiled clingfilm and leave to rise for a further 30 minutes until the dough doubles.

To make the piping paste, mix the flour, sugar and water to form a paste and spoon into a paper icing bag. Pipe the paste over the buns to form crosses. Bake in a preheated oven, 200˚C (400˚F), Gas Mark 6, for 30–35 minutes until risen and golden, covering the tin loosely with foil if the buns start to brown.

Meanwhile, to make the apricot glaze, put the jam in a small saucepan with the lemon juice and water and heat gently until the jam melts. Increase the heat and boil for 1 minute, remove from the heat and press through a fine sieve. Remove the buns from the oven, brush each bun with apricot glaze and transfer to a wire rack to cool.

Easter Nests

Makes 12
Preparation time 35 minutes,
  plus cooling
Cooking time 25 minutes

12 Chocolate Orange
  Cupcakes (see page 51)

Chocolate fudge frosting
100 g (3½ oz) plain or milk
  chocolate, chopped
2 tablespoons milk
50 g (2 oz) unsalted butter
75 g (3 oz) icing sugar

To decorate
200 g (7 oz) flaked chocolate
  bars, cut into 2.5 cm (1 inch)
  lengths
36 candy-covered chocolate
  mini eggs

To make the chocolate fudge frosting, put the chocolate, milk and butter in a small, heavy-based saucepan and heat gently, stirring, until the chocolate and butter have melted. Remove from the heat and stir in the icing sugar until smooth. Spread the cooled frosting over the tops of the cooled cakes using a small palette knife, spreading it right to the edges.

To decorate, cut the short lengths of flaked chocolate bars lengthways into thin 'shards'. Arrange the chocolate shards around the edges of the cakes, pressing them into the icing at different angles to resemble birds' nests. Pile 3 eggs into the centre of each 'nest'.

Birthday Cake

Serves 12
Preparation time 25 minutes
Cooking time 35–40 minutes

175 g (6 oz) soft margarine,
  plus extra for greasing
175 g (6 oz) caster sugar
2 teaspoons vanilla essence
300 g (10 oz) self-raising flour
2 teaspoons baking powder
3 eggs
50 g (2 oz) ground rice
150 ml (¼ pint) low-fat natural
  yogurt
175 g (6 oz) strawberries,
  finely chopped

To fill and decorate
300 ml (½ pint) double cream
3 tablespoons strawberry jam
250 g (8 oz) strawberries,
  hulled and sliced

Grease 2 x 20 cm (8 inch) loose-bottomed, round cake tins lightly with margarine, and line the bases of the tins with nonstick baking paper. Cream the margarine and sugar in a food processor with the vanilla essence until smooth. Sift the flour and baking powder over the creamed mixture, add the eggs, ground rice and yogurt and whiz together until creamy. Fold the strawberries into the mixture.

Divide the mixture between the prepared tins and bake in a preheated oven, 180°C (350°F), Gas Mark 4, for 35–40 minutes until risen, golden and springy to the touch. Allow to cool in the tins for 10 minutes before removing to a wire rack to cool completely. Remove the baking paper.

Whip the cream to soft peaks. Cut the top off one of the cakes to level it, spread with the jam and then half the cream to the edges. Scatter with two-thirds of the strawberries. Place the other cake on top and spread with the remaining cream. Scatter with the remaining strawberries and add candles.

Index

Acknowledgements

Photography © Octopus Publishing Group/ Marie Louise Avery 132 (top right), 140, 145, a146, 150;/Marie Louise Avery and Olivier Maynard 2 (bottom right), 21, 26, 55 60 (top right), 69, 74, 82;/ Jean Cazals 19;/ Stephen Conroy 8, 10 (top right and bottom left), 15, 18, 24, 28, 36 (top right), 56, 59, 64, 85, 102, 104, 108 (top left, top right and bottom right), 115, 116, 120, 124, 126, 129, 131, 152 (bottom right), 156, 158, 169, 169, 170, 182;/ Will Heap 86 (bottom left), 88, 112, 118, 122;/ William Lingwood 10 (top left), 23;/ David Munns 6, 7, 17, 36 (top left and bottom right), 39, 42, 44, 46, 47, 49, 50, 99, 132 (bottom left), 141, 143, 149, 172 (top left), 179;/ Lis Parsons 2 (top left), 10 (bottom right), 13, 53, 79, 108 (bottom left), 110, 172 (bottom right), 175, 176, 180, 187;/ Gareth Sambidge 172 (top right), 186;/ William Shaw 2 (top right), 14, 36 (bottom left), 41, 60 (bottom left), 70, 73, 76, 80, 86 (top right and bottom right), 95, 96, 132 (top left and bottom right), 134, 136, 138;/ Ian Wallace 2 (bottom left), 9, 31, 32, 34, 60 (top left and bottom right), 63, 66, 86 (top left), 90, 93, 100, 107, 151, 152 (top left, top right, bottom left), 154, 163, 164, 167, 172 (bottom left), 185